STARTLE *and* ILLUMINATE

STARTLE

and

ILLUMINATE

Carol Shields on Writing

EDITED BY
ANNE GIARDINI AND NICHOLAS GIARDINI

RANDOM HOUSE CANADA

PUBLISHED BY RANDOM HOUSE CANADA

Copyright © 2016 Carol Shields Literary Trust
Introduction Copyright © 2016 Anne Giardini and Nicholas Giardini
Foreword Copyright © 2016 Jane Urquhart

www.penguinrandomhouse.ca

Random House Canada and colophon are registered trademarks.

Library and Archives Canada Cataloguing in Publication

Shields, Carol, 1935–2003, author
    Startle and illuminate : Carol Shields on writing / Carol Shields, Anne Giardini, Nicholas Giardini.

Includes index.
Issued in print and electronic formats.

ISBN 978-0-345-81594-1
eBook ISBN 978-0-345-81596-5

    1. Authorship. 2. Reading. 3. Shields, Carol, 1935–2003—Technique. I. Giardini, Anne, author II. Giardini, Nicholas, 1991–, author III. Title.

PN151.S53 2016   808.02   C2015-906419-8

Book design by Rachel Cooper
Cover photograph © Neil Graham
Printed and bound in the United States of America

10 9 8 7 6 5 4 3 2 1

Penguin
Random House
RANDOM HOUSE CANADA

For Don—husband, father and grandfather

CONTENTS

I've always believed fiction to be about redemption,
about trying to see why people are the way they are.
CAROL SHIELDS

FOREWORD

BY JANE URQUHART

I CANNOT RECALL WITH ANY ACCURACY WHEN I FIRST MET Carol Shields. Was it at a book-tour reading in Winnipeg in the early 1990s, or that time at a Toronto Festival when she introduced me to her sister? Or was it at a prize dinner, or something similar? She was that essential, positive person who, had she not existed, I might have had to invent. I still can't believe that she hadn't been there forever, and wouldn't be there forever. I already knew and loved her work—*Swann, Various Miracles*—before we met; that much I am sure of. And there is no question that familiarity with the work always makes one feel a kinship when one is lucky enough to come to know the author. But in Carol's case there was more, much more. It was in her voice, not just in her writing voice, which was undeniably extraordinary, but in the sound of her voice. Her speech was bell-like, musical, and what she said would sing in the mind long after she had said it. She still speaks to me, an encouraging whisper in my ear. I quote her shamelessly, and as often as I can. There isn't a distant acquaintance who hasn't heard me utter a sentence that begins with the words, "Well, Carol always said that…"

This book is a treasure, in that it captures the sound of that voice, that other, non-fiction voice, the voice of the spoken word. It is the voice that Carol used in conversation with her fellow authors and with her friends, the voice with which she pondered aloud what it is to be a writer. How we are drawn to use narrative, to examine and transform life, to revel in the construction of a sentence. Or what trails we might blaze in order "to shorten the distance between what is privately felt and universally known." It is the voice she used to tell us that being on the edge actually gave us an edge, and that absolutely nothing should silence or stop us, that there were no viable rules about who should or shouldn't be heard, and that there was never a story too small or ordinary, or a point of view too marginal, to be examined. "There is no such thing as a boring life," she once said. Even people bored by life were interesting to her. Read the obituaries of so-called ordinary people, she instructs in these pages; pay attention. "I wanted Mrs. Turner," she writes to a student, "with all her particles of difference, to shine."

Carol was a gifted eavesdropper and voyeur. Her ear and her gaze were both empathetic and penetrating. She was drawn to the stories of strangers and, while not unsympathetic concerning these stories, she was never sentimental. She was as fascinated by the dark as she was by the light. In these pages she explores the sun and the shadows of the writing life, and she invites us to join her in that exploration.

A benign, though insistent, inquirer, Carol was relentlessly curious. About everything. "Why have you never written about your first husband's death?" she once asked me. I had no answer to this question. "Well," she said, "I think you should write about it now." The gift of Carol's advice, on any subject, was delivered with such positive energy that it was impossible not to take it and be grateful. I am not certain that "advice" is the right word, in fact, for it was dispatched so gracefully that it was more along the lines of wise observation followed by generous encouragement. Thanks to this book, these wise observations and that generous encouragement will be more widely disseminated.

Carol wanted to know what made writers tick. She wanted to reflect upon what drew her to her own work and, at the same time, speculate about what it might be that would help another along the path to his or hers. Writing, in all its guises, or even the possibility of writing, fully delighted her. All through her career, her life, she amazed us with her eagerness and passion. The title of this book is perfect. Carol always startled us, in the best of ways, and then she illuminated. And she still does.

GENEROSITY, TIME AND FINAL ADVICE

BY ANNE GIARDINI

AS THE AUTHOR OF TWO NOVELS, WITH ANOTHER ON THE WAY, I am asked from time to time for advice on writing, finding time to write, starting, plotting, forming characters, finishing, publishing, and other aspects of getting one's words into print. A year or two ago, it struck me that some of the best advice I had received was from my mother, Carol Shields, and that this advice might be useful to others. My son Nicholas was living in Ottawa at the time and I asked if he would dig into his grandmother's papers in the literary archives at Library and Archives Canada to see what he could find on the subject of writing. He found a lot. There were more ideas about the process of writing than I had heard from my mother directly, and all of this was new to him. We jointly decided to create this book. In the course of working with Nicholas, and later our editors, Anne Collins and Amanda Lewis, I began to see that this book could never possibly be complete. I regularly run into people who delight in telling me—as I delight in hearing—ideas and advice they received from my mother about how to be a better writer (as well as how to be a better person, but that would be another book, and no doubt also illuminating).

Throughout her writing life, Carol shared generously from her store of wisdom on writing; some learned from others, much of it her own discovery.

We weren't, however, generally an advice-giving family, at least among ourselves—although, perhaps because it was so rare, we didn't mind receiving counsel from each other. The rare time we were tempted or solicited to dispense any opinion that might be construed as advice, we tended to water it down to the point of homeopathy and then administer it aslant, in a what-do-I-know-take-it-or-leave-it manner. We were not very much invested in our advice being followed; in fact, I think we were relieved when it was not, since we were then absolved of any responsibility for the consequences. But my four siblings and I did read and comment on what our mother was writing because she invited us to do so. She wasn't secretive. She encouraged us to delve into her manuscripts and mark or suggest at will. Why she did this is clear to me now: she loved writing and thought we would too. I sometimes joke that writing is the family business in the same way that the butcher's children might take up exsanguination, skinning, eviscerating, splitting, boning, cutting and trimming. When she asked us to witness the creation of her work, my mother was also welcoming us to consider taking it up ourselves. By opening the process to our view, she reduced the mystique of writing without in any way minimizing the wonder of making narrative from words, imagination, paper and print. Inoculated in this way, I felt fairly confident as a writer from earliest childhood, and later became a columnist and then a novelist, although my mother died before my first novel was written. My sister Sara has become an accomplished poet, essayist and writer of children's books and has even, in some years, accomplished the feat of living from the proceeds of her pen.

The best advice my mother gave directly to me on the subject of writing was this: to write as if you were spilling your story into the ear of a perfect listener, and in as direct and unmediated a way as possible. She made a gesture as she said this, placing two fingers against her lips, and then turning her hand and reaching toward that perfect ear, close and avid. Like many of the ideas in this book, this advice might apply as much to navigating life as to arranging words on a page or screen. Every storyteller, speechmaker or dinner table conversationalist should know this trick of speaking authentically, without artifice or impediment, to an enchanted listener. I wrote my first novel in this way, imagining that I was telling it straight into the ear of one of my sisters, who knew nothing of it during the writing—that was not the point. It was her imaginary ear I needed, and her imagined response. This approach completely changed how I wrote, since I could sense my sister's reactions to every word as I typed. This sister is a good listener, with a keen sense of narrative and a fine and discerning sensibility. I also commandeer her acute eye before I allow myself to purchase any item of clothing. This is, it seems, a useful and expanding exercise, seeing, hearing, processing through the borrowed senses of a trusted other.

Freydis Welland, daughter of Joan Austen-Leigh, and a niece of Jane Austen several generations removed, became a well-loved friend of my mother, and since she kept impeccable notes, was one of our most reliable sources during the collection of this book. "I have no patience," she records my mother saying in October 2002, "with those who think novels write themselves. They don't. They are not a mystical thing. But this last novel [*Unless*] almost seemed to. It grew organically."

Revising, because it is close, precise and persnickety, is frequently the opposite of writing, which can—at least on the good days—flow along like water. Freydis recalled my mother referring to the reworking of *Unless* as a process during which she had "taken it apart with jeweller's tweezers." Carol described to her the satisfying challenge of working through a complex paragraph or sentence, ending up with one "that bulges out in the middle and comes safely to completion." In a letter to Freydis—my mother kept up a wide-ranging, lively correspondence with friends, readers, fellow writers and others—Carol referred to Virginia Woolf, who wrote this, of George Eliot: "The width of the prospect, the large strong outlines of the principal features, the ruddy light of her early books, the searching power and reflective richness of the later tempt us to linger and expatiate beyond our limits."

"Ruddy light, yes," my mother added. "We must make sure there is enough ruddy light in our books to keep them glowing." Her wish as a reader and writer was for books that startle, illuminate, gleam with internal light.

All of us, five children—a son, John (1958), me (1959), then Catherine (1962), Meg (1964) and Sara (1968)—saw our mother writing, and we read her work, as she invited us to do, often at its earliest stages. As children and then teenagers we watched her type the poems that won her first prize in the CBC's Young Writer's Competition in 1964 and found publication in journals and in her own collections, and then write the novels, short stories, plays and non-fiction that earned her recognition and awards around the world, among them the Canadian Authors' Association Award for Best Novel (1976); first prize in the CBC's Annual Literary Competition (1983); a Canadian National Magazine Award (1985); the Arthur Ellis Award for Best Canadian Mystery (1988); the Marian Engel Award for body of work (1990); the Governor General's Literary Award for Fiction (1993); the Canadian Booksellers Association Prize (1994); the National Book Critics Circle Award for Fiction (1994); the Pulitzer Prize for Fiction (1995); the Orange Prize (1998); the Prix de Lire (France) (1998); the Charles Taylor Prize (2002); and the Ethel Wilson Prize (2003).

Carol was often ahead of her time in discerning trends and interests that would fascinate and delight readers. She referred, for example, to a subset of her short stories as her "little weirdies." I wonder what she would have made of the emergence of what is called the "new weird" category of literature. Hers tended less, perhaps, to discomfiting ends than the modern new weird, which often strives to unsettle. An example is her story "Flatties: Their Various Forms and Uses," which describes a world in which children collecting eggs "never stumble, no egg is ever broken."

Dropped Threads, an anthology about women's experiences that Carol co-edited, became a bestseller, to the (happy) surprise of her publisher.*

Carol and her collaborator, Marjorie Anderson, had smartly seen the need for a book that examined the gaps in what women write about or say aloud. There was, as they discerned, a desire to read about defining moments rarely aired in common discourse, truths seldom shared, subjects that had not yet found a place.

---

* Anne Collins, who edited *Dropped Threads*, remembers it receiving mixed reviews until Shelagh Rogers featured it on an hour-long coffee klatch on CBC's *This Morning*. Two days later, the book sprang onto the bestseller lists and stayed there for over forty weeks.

In an interview in *The Vancouver Sun* in 2003, a few months before my mother's death in July of that year, I mentioned reading my mother's writing when I was growing up, as the pages stacked up beside her typewriter. "It was sort of like running my fingers through silk," I said. Then I described to the reporter how, after I moved away from home, it felt odd that some of her books came out before I had the chance to run my fingers through them. They seemed to me to have come out of thin air. I missed witnessing their creation.

We children did from time to time, despite the family aversion to giving advice, tell Carol what we thought about what she was writing. Youth. Hubris. Families.

I have an undated, typed letter from my mother when she was writing her novel *Swann* (1987) that contains an uncharacteristically detailed request for advice. I was in my early twenties then, and interested in a central character in *Swann*, Sarah Maloney, a young American feminist academic. In her letter, my mother wrote:

I'll thank you in advance, as they say, for reading my manuscript which is already on its way to you. I'm enclosing a fiver for return postage. Here are some of the things I'd like to know. Anything you find irritating? anything over-written? not sufficiently developed? overly clue-dropping? characters acting out of character?—not that this can't happen. And, the big question, what do you imagine might happen next? I am not going to begin my edit of the last section until I hear from you. I am at that point that I reached in The Box Garden where I didn't know if I'd revealed too much or too little. But the mystery element of this novel is not its main focus, as you will see, but more of a diversion. The focus, I like to think, is Appearance and Reality. Rather pompous that.

Also interested in different ways of defining human personality, and different ways of formulating that definition—which is why the narrative approach is different in the four sections. The final section, as I think I told you, is a screenplay. (Still a little wobbly.) I'll send it to you as soon as I hear from you because I know you'll have suggestions. The [photocopied] manuscript is already so marked up it won't do any good to write on it—I'd never find it. Perhaps you could use little posties (those yellow things).

In handwriting, she added in the left margin:

Sarah (recently renamed Sarah Maloney) is *supposed* to be slightly irritating. She irritates *herself.* Does this come across sufficiently?

In a later letter she wrote:

I want to thank you again for all your comments about the novel. I truly believe you've made me take a second look and see what was wrong. Your comments, which echoed Catherine's [one of my sisters], have resulted in a reworking of the Sarah section. I took your advice about the beginning, and retouched, if that is the word, many other spots. I think part of the problem was a kind of heartlessness about other women, Rose particularly, perceived in cliché terms, slickly shallow. My dive into style, as well as my attempt to write "young," led me astray I think. I also altered the Cruzzi sections as you suggested, which made a much more logical and appealing sequence. The whole thing was mailed off to my editor yesterday—we will have next Saturday in Toronto to go over it detail by detail. When Sara [another sister] read your letter she said, "That's just what I felt." All things considered, I trust you "blood critics" much more than these disembodied Toronto lit sorts. At any rate, I do send thanks.

Far more often, as I was relieved to see when I revisited our letters, I sent letters of validation. My mother needed validation, after all, as all writers do.

From a letter to me dated October 20, 1985:

Thank you for your kind words about Various Miracles, especially "ferny head," because that was a phrase I had to defend when my editor, over the phone, wanted it out—thought it meaningless. (Fath [my father, Donald Shields] agrees.)

* * *

This book, *Startle and Illuminate*, covers how my mother went about writing, and what she thought about how others might write better. I am also often asked how, with five small children, my mother found the *time* to write.

When my mother graduated in 1957 from Hanover College, a small liberal arts school on the Ohio River near Madison, Indiana, she was already a promising writer, and had, as it happens, merited her college's top writing prize. However, she did not receive it. Instead, she was asked if she would mind if the committee gave it not to her, but to the young male student who had come in second. He would, after all, have to earn his living, and the prize would help him to do so. My mother, aged twenty-one, agreed—blithely as she told the story, although I do sometimes wonder. She was about to be married. She knew she would have children—she went on to have five inside the next ten years. What use would a writing prize be to her as a young wife and mother? Or so she thought. Timing may not be everything, but it is a lot. The mid-1950s was a time when women were treated, as the author Anne Fine has put it, much like a "pleat in the economy, taken in and let out as circumstances change."

"Time" was the theme of the convocation from Hanover College, the address delivered by a popular math professor. What he said to his young and eager audience on that bright June day was this:

Tempus fugit. Time flies.

My mother remembered it as a warning that, unless the graduates before him seized the moment—in fact seized every moment— their lives would get away from them. Their days and years would be eroded, erased, wasted. Thrown away through carelessness...lost. As a result, in the years that immediately followed, my mother said,

> years in which I might be changing diapers, washing floors, driving
> children here and there, sewing, shopping, cooking meals, writing
> thank you notes, weeding the garden, reading a little poetry
> on the sly...those words would occasionally come back to me:
> "*Tempus fugit.*"

Then her life changed. Slowly at first, but significantly. In 1962 after we moved to Manchester where my father was doing post-doctoral work, the British magazine *The Storyteller* accepted a short story, the first publication for which she was paid. *The Storyteller* was a monthly magazine sold mainly in train stations to travellers. The British Broadcasting Corporation also bought a short story from her. The story, "For Business Reasons," was broadcast in March of 1962.

Carol wrote these stories in the moments she squeezed from her busy days raising her family. Back in Canada, starting in the mid-1960s, she also wrote and published poems. In 1976, when her youngest child was eight and she was forty-two, she published her first novel, *Small Ceremonies*. She went on to publish a number of collections of poetry and short stories, as well as more novels, plays and non-fiction.

But how did she find time, Terry Gross of NPR's *Fresh Air* asked her in 2002.

"Everyone asks me this," Carol said.

But I didn't have a job. I didn't write until [the children] went to school, and I didn't write on weekends and I didn't write in the evening. None of this was possible. But I used to try to get that hour just before they came home for lunch, 11 to 12. You know, got all those socks picked up, etc. and then I tried to write a couple of pages. That was all I ever asked myself to do. Then sometimes, in the afternoon, before they came home from school, I would get back to those two pages, and maybe have a chance to do them over again. But I really only had about an hour or an hour and a half a day. This was how I organized my time, that I would give myself one or two pages a day, and if I didn't get to my two pages, I would get into bed at night with one of those thick yellow tablets of lined paper, and I would do two quick pages and then turn off the light. I did this for nine months, and at the end of nine months, I had a novel. I could see how it could be done in little units. I thought of it like boxcars. I had nine boxcars, and each chapter had a title starting with September, and then October, November, December, so it was a very easy structure for someone writing a first novel to follow.

What I learned from my mother about the art of finding time is this: find *any* time that you might happen to be able to muster, and structure your task so that it fits into that time in a way that allows you to finish what you want to achieve. Years later, I wrote my own first two novels in part on a laptop at hockey rinks. That was the time available to me. (Not incidentally, the purring, glowing warmth of my computer softened the dim, cold arenas where house league hockey games are played. Other parents would kindly alert me if it looked likely that whichever child was playing at the time might be about to do something that I should attend to so that I could comment on it later.)

There may not be a perfect time, and there may not be as much of it as we would like, but if we can find some bits of it, and organize them in a way that makes sense, then we may be able to turn those scraps and moments into something enduring—a poem, a story, a memoir, a novel. The days cannot be stretched, but they can be shaped.

In part from my mother's experience, in part from my own, and in part from observing other busy and successful people, particularly creative people, I have seen over and over that the nature of time requires that we consciously shape our goals, and that we take up the things that are most important to us—our friends, our work, our families, our art—and fold them like origami into the time we have; or alternatively, that we bend the time we have to those important tasks.

It helps if we start by reframing our perspective of work as overwhelming, and of time as inherently limited. When we come from a mindset of scarcity, life will feel scant. When we come from a perspective of plenty, we encounter life as abundant. Time is like this too. We should treat it as precious and *profuse*, not inadequate.

The reframing has to do with changing challenges—such as where to find time—into advantages, such as, how will I make the best use of the time that is demonstrably available to me?

Each second, each hour, each day, week, month and year of our existence is, after all, a miracle. And each, as that math professor urged, is to be seized. But time is not in fact fleeting or sparse, not if we treat it as expansive and abundant and as generously given to us to spend as we choose.

It helps, as I mentioned, to think of time in a structured way. One way is to consider time and the tasks that fill it as boxcars, the metaphor my mother thought of when constructing her first novel. Have you ever been stuck at a railway crossing while a train went by, seemingly endless, passenger car or freight car after tanker car, the looked-for caboose never quite coming into sight? Perhaps especially in North America, who has *not* been stuck like this on the near side of the tracks? Time is like that train. This moment connects to an almost endless chain in past and future. The days are expansive. The train is long. The caboose is still a ways away. When we shape our time or work or both—into boxcars, or whatever segmentation works best for you—we find that we *do* have the time we need to start, create, write. Not every day. Not every year. (My mother said she lost a year every time our family moved.) But we have more control over time than we often allow ourselves to believe.

In a commencement address that Carol gave to the class of 1996 at the University of British Columbia, she reflected on the anxiety that had been planted by that math professor's advice.

Time was hurrying by. Brushing past me. I could almost hear the flapping of the winged chariot. My little life was left behind in the dust. I was standing still or so I thought. The words *Tempus fugit*, whenever I paused to recollect my graduation day, spooked me, scared me. I was persuaded that I had failed, because I was not filling every day with accomplishment. I was not pushing forward and making the most of my allotted time on earth.

But by 1996, likely much earlier, Carol had achieved an important insight. Time *was* precious but it was not fleeting. She had raised a large family. She had published dozens of books. She had travelled. She had read. She had sustained a long marriage and empowering, delight-filled friendships. She had talked and laughed and shared ideas with thousands of people as friend, mother, teacher, mentor. She had written letters, scrubbed floors, dried tears, wrapped and unwrapped presents, picked flowers, baked pies, argued, danced, slept, wept— experienced that full range of what life has to offer. Her conclusion?

Tempus does not *fugit.*

Here's what she told the students that day:

Time is not cruel. Given the good luck of a long healthy life, as most of us have, we have plenty. Plenty of time. We have time to try our new selves. Time to experiment. Time to dream and drift. Time even to waste. Fallow time. Shallow time.

We'll have good years and bad years. And we can afford both. Every hour will not be filled with meaning and accomplishment as the world measures such things but there will be compensating hours so rich, so full, so humanly satisfying that we will become partners with time and not victims of it.

Most of us end up seeing our lives not as an ascending line of achievement but as a series of highly interesting chapters.

We might not have the good luck of a long healthy life. My mother didn't. She died on a beautiful summer day thirteen years ago, a few days after her sixty-eighth birthday, of breast cancer that had metastasized to her liver and elsewhere. Some of us won't make it that far. Some of us will see the other side of a hundred; so save your pennies, just in case—they might have to last you a long time.

All of us can and should live in time fully but without the anxiety of it running out on us. We created time. The physicists tell us it exists as a flow, to the extent it does exist, only because we serve as a point of reference. In that case, there is no reason for us to be its victims. I like my mother's formulation very much—we should instead assume our rightful role as *partners* of time. We measure, slice, dice, sell, count up, monetize and commodify time, but in doing so we are conscious actors, making decisions about how it should be used and spent.

An image of this partnership came to me when I was reading Helen Macdonald's remarkable book set in and around Cambridge, England, called *H Is for Hawk*. This memoir tells of the difficult, painstaking conditioning of a hawk by Macdonald, who has suffered a near collapse after the death of her beloved father, a photojournalist.

In falconry, or its hawk equivalent, austringery, neither owner nor bird is a victim or master of the other. They become partners. You see a falconer or austringer holding a falcon or hawk on a gloved hand joined by a creance, the long light cord used to tether a bird during training, and you understand how they work together, toward death—because falcons and hawks are birds of prey after all.

As my mother's daughter, I see time in that way, that same linked partnership, the bird on our arm ready for flight, toward death, yes, but while we are tethered together fully alive and calling on each other to live fully in time—intelligently, fiercely.

The last bit of advice I directly received from my mother may have been given about two years after her death. I was booked for an early morning television interview at the start of a tour to promote my first book, *The Sad Truth about Happiness*, and was waiting in the wings of the set, about to walk on to join the host. I was jet-lagged. Nervous. Anxious about my three small children at home. I felt a light pressure on my shoulder and I had an impression of my mother's voice in my left ear.

"Be serene" was what I heard.

I am under no illusions about ghosts or spirits, but I know it to be true that sometimes the mind delivers comforts or reassurance that feel poised on the far margin of reasonable explanation.

We hope this book finds its way into the hands of other grateful writers, perhaps also at a time of need, who will have the great good fortune, as we have had, to hear and be encouraged by that same voice.

COMING TO KNOW MY GRANDMOTHER
THROUGH HER WRITING

BY NICHOLAS GIARDINI

I DON'T RECALL MY GRANDMOTHER AS A GIVER OF ADVICE. I remember walks outside, mosquito-bite kisses, cups of tea, interesting conversations that left me with lingering questions, hugs that lasted a long time, and love. My grandmother clearly loved all her grandchildren and I felt lucky to be among them. She died when I was eleven years old so I was too young to have a perception of her as anything other than a grandma—my grandma.

It wasn't until a few years later, when I entered high school, that I began to read my grandmother's stories. I came across the first story in the middle of one of my English class anthologies. I had always understood that my grandma was a writer, but I had felt too young or too daunted to try to read her books. That first short story I came upon was all it took to make me braver. I skipped the assigned reading that day and instead read my first Carol Shields story, "Weather." And was hooked. That year I tore through my grandmother's bibliography. (I read indiscriminately at the time, of course, spacing out her novels with sci-fi and the novels of Stephen King.) I started with *Unless*. I laughed at the funny parts, cried at the sad parts, and cringed through the sexy parts. In reading, I developed a separate and new perception of my grandmother as an author.

My mother, Anne Giardini, proposed this book project to me on Mother's Day in 2013, although I doubt this date had any significance for her. My mother thinks about her own mother daily (hourly?) and I suspect she had been thinking about this book for some time before she shared the idea with me. I was living in Ottawa and finishing my undergraduate degree. My mother told me that Carol's papers were housed in Library and Archives Canada in downtown Ottawa—dozens, perhaps hundreds of boxes of material shipped there over many years. My mum imagined a book—this book—that featured my grandmother's writing advice, in her own words. Would I be interested, she asked, in going through the fonds in the archives and seeing what I could find?

Several weeks later, my mother came to Ottawa for work meetings. She carved out some hours with me and described, in detail, what she was envisioning. Her ideas went beyond a single book of writing advice. Could we establish a writing prize? Hold a contest to pair Carol Shields' poetry with art pieces? Establish an annual Daisy Goodwill Flett Day during which women who were absent from the centre of our collective lives might be honoured? My mum was focused, ferocious, and determined, a side of her I wasn't often privy to. Her excitement stirred my enthusiasm and I was immensely compelled to discover what the collection actually contained.

We filled out some forms and waited a couple of days, after which I was astonished to receive permission to enter the archives and see the Carol Shields materials. I felt the same thrill of potential discovery I had felt when that high school anthology fell open to the words: "By Carol Shields." Thanks to the help of skilled staff, I found the material well organized and easy enough to go through. Catherine Hobbs, the archivist who has been responsible for processing and organizing the material since 1997, walked me though what was available. She showed me the finding aids that she had prepared and advised me to be meticulous in recording what I found and where I found it. I had never been particularly organized, but, for fear of letting my mum (and Catherine) down, I kept careful track each day I spent there.

Finding aids are like a restaurant menu. I picked out everything that I thought would be useful or interesting. I was able to order up letters, essays, drafts and magazine clippings, some with pen notes jotted in the margins and some covered in highlighter. There, in the literal and figurative margins, I began to build what felt like a personal connection with my grandmother. I began to see who she was and how important she had been to many other people, even loved by them. On my first day in the archives, as I greedily thumbed through the available materials, images of my own mother from my childhood kept coming to mind. Still. Distracted. Gazing lovingly. I hoped that in addition to the advice I was seeking I would find something that could help me understand the origins of that kind of love.

I requested anything I thought could be interesting and what I found slowly humanized my grandma. My notes from that time are littered with paragraphs and turns of phrase I enjoyed. One of the first letters I read was from Arlette and Bill Baker, written in 1994. They had read a travel article Carol had written and invited her and my grandfather, Don, to give them a call or drop by if they ever found themselves in a particular part of France. The Bakers had never met either of my grandparents. The four became friends, and, after the deaths of Carol and Bill, Don and Arlette began a lasting relationship. One that began with that single letter.

I read the response to an "audacious" request from Toronto's Book City. Book City had written for permission to put Carol's profile on a shopping bag as part of a series on Canadian authors. My grandma wrote a polite note declining the invitation.

I found letters of congratulations from fans and acquaintances. I hadn't before considered how many people actually take the time to write to authors. It seemed that my grandma had a talent for making people instantly feel at ease. My favourite of these comes from Bonnie, who wrote to my grandmother shortly after *The Stone Diaries* won the Pulitzer Prize in 1995:

> I have had a couple of excruciating evenings in T.O. this past year,
> wishing I was young and beautiful, or outrageous, or above it all;
> anything but what I am. Having someone look above my head to
> see if there is someone more important to talk to is like a return
> to some terrible childhood. Although it's not the real champions
> who do this. . . . And I distinctly remember a solid gaze from you
> during a reception a few years ago at the Globe Theatre in Regina.
> I would guess you have looked at many people this way.
>
> No one will be looking beyond your head now. Good on ya.

Another of my favourite letters was from a bemused man named Larry Weller, the same name of the protagonist of *Larry's Party*. In an eloquent, handwritten letter, Larry expresses his shock to find that he has become the hero of a novel. ("How did you know? When were you watching?")

I also came across correspondence between my mum and her mother. There were letters about family, letters about work and letters about writing. I found a lovely letter from my mum detailing my growth as a toddler:

Nicholas is UNFOLDING these days before our eyes. He has a
wonderful analytic dispassionate intelligence which awes me. I
told you I thought I might love them too much, but I think I meant
Nick. He is so lovely, thoughtful, watchful and intelligent that I
fear that to love him so much must tempt fate.

These nuggets of personal interest were interspersed with the material that will follow. I found hundreds of pages that included writing advice. I read through years of correspondence between my grandmother and a number of writers: some experienced, and some trying to figure out where to start or where to go next. I read course notes and assignments from when my grandma was preparing and teaching creative writing classes. I read speeches that were read to graduates and talks given at conferences. Across continents, people sought out my grandmother to hear her ideas and learn from her. The scale at which she was sought after and adored was enormous, too big for me to comprehend. I learned of her humility and her sense of self and her interest in others. My grandmother wrote back to almost everyone who contacted her, and her letters show unfailing care and respect; the same woman who had read to me at night and taken me for hot chocolate in the morning, and who had seemed to have all the time in the world for me.

In order to begin reading my grandmother's stories in high

school, I needed the push of discovering her name in that anthology. My mum provided a similar push for me to go to the archives and learn about my grandmother in a different light. At the time that my mum proposed the project, I had been aware of the existence of the collection for a few years. I even once prepared an application to view the material, but I never followed through. For four years, those files existed literally blocks from my home and I never once approached the building. I first needed to find a reason to go there. All I needed was to have that first phone call with my mum, to hear her determination to understand Carol, and her determination for me to understand as well. She could have hired a researcher, but instead she asked me. She wanted me to see a new side of my grandmother.

I don't think my perception of my grandmother will stop growing any time soon. Just recently, one of my mother's sisters, my aunt Meg, asked me to digitize a boxful of two-reel home movies from the 1950s and '60s, recording life at my grandparents' homes in Ottawa and Toronto, and so I've also had the chance to immerse myself in this silent history. I've been incredibly lucky to learn about her in these movies, and in photos, in her papers and in her advice.

The advice on writing I found in the archives is, as it happens, advice I very much want to take. The writer in me—and there is one—has countless areas in which to grow and mature, but what I read while doing research for this book may have given me some of what I need if I decide, as I just might, to start writing myself.

~ 1 ~

WRITERS ARE READERS FIRST

I'VE NEVER BEEN ABLE TO SEPARATE MY READING AND MY WRITING life. As you know, there is a time in our early reading lives when we read anything, when we are unsupervised, when we are bonded to the books we read. When we are innocent of any kind of critical standard, so innocent and avid and open that we don't even bother to seek out special books, but read instead those books that happen to lie within easy reach, the family books, the in-house books. These books have a way of entering our bodies more simply and completely than library books, for example, which are chosen, or school texts that are imposed.

It's a literary cliché, largely aristocratic, largely male, that writers in their young years are "given the run of their father's library." You imagine oak panelling, a fire, a set of leather-bound volumes, Shakespeare, of course, but also the Greek dramatists, the Latin poets, the Fathers of the Church, Dickens, Scott, an almost exclusively masculine offering with little visible connection between book and reader.

My parents' library was a corner of the sunroom, a four-shelf bookcase stained to look like red maple that had been thrown in with the purchase of the 1947 edition of the *World Book Encyclopedia.* There was also room on those shelves for a set of *Journeys through Bookland* and two volumes of poetry, the works of James Whitcomb Riley, who I thought was a great poet before I went to university and found he wasn't, and *A Heap o' Livin'* by Edgar A. Guest. The rest of the shelf space, only a few inches, was filled with my parents' childhood books.

My father was represented by half a dozen Horatio Alger titles, *Luck and Pluck, Ragged Dick, Try and Trust,* and so on, which I read, loved, and never thought to condemn for didacticism, for didn't I attend a didactic Methodist Sunday School, sit in a didactically charged classroom, absorb the didacticism of my well-meaning parents? This was the natural way of the world, half of humanity bent on improving the other half. Nor did it seem strange that I, in the 1940s and '50s, should be reading books directed at a late nineteenth and early twentieth century audience. I scarcely noticed this time fissure, entering instead a seamless, timeless universe, scrubbed of such topical events as the wars, elections, social upheavals with which we mark off periods of history. Occasional archaisms were easily overleapt, since a child's world is largely a matter of missing pieces anyway, or concepts only dimly grasped.

Horatio Alger aside, it was mainly the books of my mother that I read, four of them in particular, two of which were Canadian, not that I noticed at the time: *Anne of Green Gables, Beautiful Joe, Helen's Babies,* and *A Girl of the Limberlost.* No Shakespeare, Hawthorne, Poe, no Virginia Woolf, Gertrude Stein, Willa Cather—just these four.

My mother, the youngest child of Swedish immigrants, grew up on an Illinois farm, attended Normal School at DeKalb and, as a young woman came to Chicago to teach school. She and three other girls roomed for a year on the third floor of the Hemingway house in Oak Park, Illinois. Ernest's sister, Sunny Hemingway, was in college, and the family needed the extra money. Ernest was away in Paris writing *The Sun Also Rises*, though my mother didn't know this of course; she only knew that his parents spoke of him coldly. "Is he an artist?" my mother once asked. "He is a time waster," his father Dr. Hemingway replied. The Hemingways were difficult landlords; they were stingy with hot water and they wouldn't allow the four young women to entertain their boyfriends, and so in a year they moved on, ending our mother's accidental brush with the world of real literature, which always excited her children more than it did her. In fact, she never read Hemingway; he was not, despite her thrilling connection, a part of her tradition.

It's easy to see what she found in *Anne of Green Gables*. She found what millions of others have found, a consciousness attuned to nature, a female model of courage, goodness, and candour, and possessed of an emotional capacity that triumphs and converts. Unlike Tom Sawyer, who capitulates to society, Anne transforms her community with her exuberant vision. She enters the story disentitled and emerges as a beloved daughter, loving friend, with a future ahead of her, and she has done it all without help: captured Gilbert Blythe, sealed her happiness, and reshuffled the values of society by a primary act of re-imagination.

And then there is *Beautiful Joe*, Marshall Saunders' enormously popular—though it's hard to see why today—1893 faux-autobiography of a mongrel dog. Like Anne Shirley, the ironically named Beautiful Joe is not conventionally beautiful, and, like Anne, his name is both his shame and his glory. Also like Anne, he is cruelly treated, but, through virtue and courage, he finds love, and he tells all this through a voice that is characterized by the most delicate, undoglike tints of feeling—though as a child I never questioned his right to a voice nor to his insights.

Nor did I worry about the sentimentality in my mother's books. Sentimentality, like coincidence, seemed to be one of the strands of American existence; it could be detected every week, after all, in the last two minutes of *Amos 'n' Andy*; it was a part of the human personality.

Anne Shirley, you remember, adored literature: "The Lady of the Lake," Thomson's *Seasons*, and something called "The Dog at His Master's Grave" from the Third Reader, all this making an eclectic sampling, typical of the randomness of early reading lists. What Anne demanded of poetry, she said, was that it give her a "crinkly feeling" up and down her back. I too was devoted to that crinkly feeling, and think, today, how different this is from Emily Dickinson's insistence that a poem must take the top of her head off. Perhaps this, then, is the difference between American and Canadian sensibility: decapitation, the big bang, versus mere vertebral crinkling.

Nellie McClung, the Canadian social activist and writer—you see how we Canadians feel obliged to stop and identify our literary figures—recounts in *her* autobiography how she burst into tears reading a piece titled "The Faithful Dog" in the Second Reader, and how her response was reinforced by a teacher who pronounced: "Here is a pupil who has both feeling and imagination, she will get a lot out of life." And we all know she did.

There was no Willa Cather on my mother's shelf, no Virginia Woolf, no George Eliot, no Jane Austen. My mother, even without dipping into these books, would have thought these writers too heavy, too intimidating for someone of her background. Always a reader, she read her way around the popular *edges* of literature. As a child I was, like my mother, approaching literature very much as an outsider, and I was intimidated by that dark dense sort of book described as a classic, though a kindly high school teacher, speaking of *Silas Marner*, demystified the term by telling us it referred to books that people have liked rather a lot for a long time. Later, though, I found that some of these so-called classics—Hemingway, to a certain extent Conrad—refused to open to me because they projected a world in which I did not hold citizenship, the world of men, action, power, ideas, politics, and war.

We use the expression "being lost in a book," but we are really closer to a state of being found. Curled up with a novel about an East Indian family, for instance, we are not so much escaping our own splintered and decentred world as we are enlarging our sense of self, our multiplying possibilities and expanded experiences. People are, after all, tragically limited: we can live in only so many places, work at a small number of jobs or professions; we can love only a finite number of people. Reading, and particularly the reading of fiction—perhaps I really do have a sales pitch here—allows us to be the other, to touch and taste the other, to sense the shock and satisfaction of otherness. A novel lets us be ourselves and yet enter another person's boundaried world, share in a private gaze between reader and writer. *Your* reading can be part of your life, and there will be times when it may be the best part.

I've always seemed to be able to take in information through print and not through other means—which is why I am so bad at languages I think. Why this should be so with some people I don't know. I rather envy people who have their senses more fully open to the world than I seem to. On the other hand, relying exclusively on one's own experience seems to me to be condemning yourself to a very narrow shelf. We can only do so much in our lives, pathetically little exposure in fact, and this seems to me to be the great benefit of fiction—that it is expansion, not escape. Shall dwell more on this—but I suppose you have to have a balance of direct and indirect experience (not sure reading is indirect however).

—*Letter to Anne Giardini*

There is nothing to fear from the new technology—but a written text, as opposed to electronic information, has formal order, tone, voice, irony, persuasion. We can inhabit a book; we can possess it and be possessed by it. The critic and scholar Martha Nussbaum believed that attentive readers of serious fiction cannot help but be compassionate and ethical citizens. The rhythms of prose train the empathetic imagination and the rational emotions.

We need literature on the page because it allows us to experience more fully, to imagine more deeply, enabling us to live more freely. Reading, you are in touch with your best self, and I think, too, that reading shortens the distance we must travel to discover that our most private perceptions are, in fact, universally felt. *Your* reading will intersect with the axis of *my* reading, and of his reading and her reading. Reading, then, offers us the ultimate website, where attention, awareness, reflection, understanding, clarity, and civility come together in a transformative experience.

It's a curious fact that once one has written a book or two, an aura of expertise is assumed. Writers are asked questions, probing questions, questions followed by short, expectant silences—which they are somehow expected to fill with pronouncements that they have not yet articulated even to themselves. What is a short story? Should a writer take political responsibility? What is the difference between prose and poetry? What is literature? What is ... life?

The question that is never asked, but which I nevertheless dread, is: why do you write? Writing after all is a rather presumptuous act, particularly since every day I meet people who have lived longer, who are wiser, who have travelled farther, have lived lives richer in adventure and courage. So isn't it a little audacious—yes, it is—to expect people to trouble themselves reading what I might write? I simply throw this out—I haven't yet found a satisfactory answer— but I suspect it would involve the belief that each of us has, however limited, a perspective that is unique. And this perspective is determined—there's no escaping it—by how and where we spent our first eighteen years or so.

Once in an interview I described Oak Park, the town where I grew up, the town where the taverns leave off and the church steeples begin, how in my childhood the population was entirely white, composed of church-going families, how teenage girls, on weekends, put on hats and white gloves and went to each other's teas, how I had never heard a really harsh four-letter word spoken aloud until I went away to university. My interviewer said,

"It sounds like growing up in a plastic bag." I said, "Yes, it was," then later regretted it.

In fact, though there was much that was narrow, smug, and hypocritical in Oak Park in the fifties, eccentricity flourished on these tree-lined streets, though it was a phenomenon I hadn't yet learned to name. The occasional iconoclasts offered surprise. Human drama existed beneath the calm republican surface, and I furthermore came to see that *all* human relationships were complex, even those in that risky literary territory known as the suburban middle class, which has been too often neglected in our fiction.

To go back to the plastic bag, there *were* a number of breathing holes, if I may use E. M. Forster's term. Fortunate glimpses of the otherness that adds subtlety and shading to the perspective we're saddled with. There was the Walsh family, who lived across the street, Frank, Liz, the twins, and Jo, who became lifelong friends and who provided what every writer requires: an image or a promise even, that there is *more*, more possibility, more ways of being, something beyond this cheerful parochial world.

There was that Oak Park trinity: school, church and library, and from the start the library claimed my primary allegiance. As a child, I read a lot but owned only three books of my own: *Under the Lilacs*, which I thought was dull, the poems of Whitcomb Riley, and *Seventeenth Summer*, which I read, I'm sure, a hundred times. There was no need to own other books, and no sense of deprivation about not having them, because we went at least once a week to the library, in my early childhood to the South Branch. And it was at the story hour, with its combination of narrative and drama, when I found pure enchantment, my first glimpse of theatre. We met in the large basement room. One of the librarians, a kindly unmarried middle-aged woman—all the librarians and schoolteachers at that time were unmarried middle-aged women—stood up and told—not read—a story. A transcendent experience. I remember one terribly cold and stormy Saturday when only four or five of us turned up. Instead of going downstairs, we sat upstairs around one of the little tables, and when I looked into the eyes of the other children there, I saw, clearly marked, the light of fanaticism. We were different. Other children loved this Saturday morning ritual, too, but we, for some reason, required it.

Every fall, Miss Mayes, the head librarian, visited the schools and talked to the children about libraries. She told us about the Dewey Decimal System. She told us the story of Abraham Lincoln walking twelve miles to return a book. She showed us how people right here in Oak Park abused books, turning down the corners of pages or employing strange inappropriate objects as bookmarks: a blue jay feather, a burnt kitchen match, and once—"once, boys and girls"—a strip of bacon. The thought of this person, and this audacious act of barbarism, thrilled me.

I remember one summer evening walking home with my stack of books, never fewer than my rightful limit, and passing a house not two blocks from the house where I lived on Kenilworth Avenue. Through the dark window screen I could hear people in the house talking—and to my astonishment, they were speaking in a foreign language. Who were these people and what did this mean? Hearing them, so unexpectedly, so close to home, I felt a bolt of happiness, the same kind of happiness I extracted from the rhythms of poetry or the turnings of the stories I read.

I should say here that I was very anxious, when I had children of my own, that they feel at home in the public library, and for quite a long period I seemed to spend an inordinate amount of time on my hands and knees groping under beds for books that were four days overdue, or four months overdue. The library fines I paid were in the double digits, and once I asked the librarian if we were the worst in the neighbourhood. No, she said, *sparing me*, there is one other family ... Once I had a phone call from the librarian in Parry Sound, Ontario, inviting me to come to give a reading. But my first thought when I heard the librarian on the line, though I'd never been to Parry Sound, was: one of the children has an overdue book.

In Oak Park, all the schools were named after famous writers. I attended Nathaniel Hawthorne Public School for the early grades, and, later, Ralph Waldo Emerson. The portraits of these two distinguished figures were displayed in the school entrance halls: bearded gentlemen wearing frock coats and cravats, immensely dignified and serious in their expression. Clearly they belonged to a privileged world, a world from which I was excluded.

Here is a confession: I loved my first grade reader, the execrable Dick and Jane, though I understand that the buoyant middle-class images are responsible for alienating and damaging generations of young Americans. I longed to embrace Mother in her apron, Father in his necktie, and I loved Dick and Jane for their clean white socks, their goodness and their almost manic enthusiasm over trifles. But I loved them chiefly because they were the key that opened the door into the world of reading, and for writers, and for many readers, the discovery of the *code* is the primary spiritual experience of childhood. I was fortunate in my teachers, a Miss Sellers in second grade who turned a corner of the classroom into a little library, furnished with tiny rugs brought from home, a bookcase and on the bookcase a small cozy lamp. When we were done with our work, we could enter this "room" and whoever was first was allowed to pull the chain on the little lamp. The effect was magic; it was a sanctuary, a stage setting, a sort of home.

I had a Miss Pelsue in fourth grade at Emerson who came to school every day at eight-thirty and read aloud to anyone who cared to come, and everyone did. And Miss Hanson—Miss Mabel Hanson, how we loved to ferret out our teachers' first names—who took me on her lap in sixth grade when I did *not* win a national penmanship award. And for seventh and eighth grade, another Mabel, Mabel Crabtree, surely that name must have been a burden for a junior high teacher to bear. She was demure, but grew vividly dramatic when teaching the Civil War. ("Oh, boys and girls," she said of the battle of Gettysburg, "oh, the stench of it.") She seemed terribly old to us, but when we rang her bell on Halloween night, she invited us in and introduced us to a Mrs. Crabtree who was much, ah, much older. It was unthinkable but true: Miss Crabtree had a mother.

In high school, there was Miss Burt who made us learn a hundred short quotations in the belief that it was good for us, and it was. And still is. Those of us in Miss Linden's senior creative writing class knew it was a privilege to be there. For this honour, we had to be specially recommended. Mr. Buskie stopped our American history class one day, saying, "I'm feeling philosophical today, and I'm going to tell you what I've been thinking." What he said was necessary and timely, about the importance of human relationships, but what lingers is the shocked relief of knowing the system could be interrupted.

I knew very early that writing was my vocation because everything else I tried—music, handicrafts, sports—went badly. Only when I was writing did the awkwardness diminish. And no one seemed offended that I wanted to be a writer. No one said, "What a crazy idea," or that ultimate put down: "Who do you think you are?" Instead teachers suggested I write the class play or submit something to the literary magazine. There was something amazing about this.

Which brings me to that question—why do writers write? There is pleasure in the making, the re-imagining, the discovery of patterns that still come together as we grow older. One of my discoveries has been the uncovering of forms that echo our realities, that interrogate the established tradition, taking liberties, and gesturing—crudely, covertly, often unconsciously—toward a dozen alternate worlds.

The resolution to become a writer formed very early in my life, but it took years for me to discover what I would write about and who my readers would be.

Several layers of trust were required before I began to find my direction. I had to learn to rely on my own voice, and after that to have faith in the value of my own experiences. At first this was frightening. The books I read as a child related daring adventures, deeds of courage. The stories took place on mountaintops or in vast cities, not in the sort of quiet green suburb where my family happened to live. It was as though there was an empty space on the bookshelf. No one seemed to talk about his void, yet I knew it was there.

Gradually I understood that the books I should write were the very books I wanted to read, the books I wasn't able to find in the library. The empty place could be closed. My small world might fill only a page at first, then several hundred pages, possibly thousands. I could make up in accuracy for what I lacked in scope, getting the details right, dividing every experience into its various shades and levels of anticipation. I could write a story, for instance, about Nathaniel Hawthorne School. About the school principal whose name was Miss Newbury (Miss Blueberry, she was called behind her back). About the chill of fear that children suffered in the schoolyard, about a fat, suffering little boy named Walter who had an English accent, and whose mother made him wear a necktie to school. About human foolishness, and about the small rescues and acts of redemption experienced along the way.

I saw that I could become a writer if I paid attention, if I was careful, if I observed the rules, and then, just as carefully, broke them.

In the books I read—and I find it hard to separate my life as a reader from that as a writer—I look first for language that cannot really exist without leaving its trace of deliberation. I want, too, the risky articulation of what I recognize but haven't yet articulated myself. And, finally, I hope for some fresh news from another country, which satisfies by its modesty, a microscopic enlargement of my vision of the world. I wouldn't dream of asking for more.

In Brief . . .

- Writers are readers first, and so all writing begins with reading.
- A writer's first books are often the ones she finds on her parents' bookshelves.
- Reading lets us be the other, touch and taste the other, sense the shock and satisfaction of otherness.
- The rhythms of prose train the empathetic imagination.
- Reading shortens the distance we must travel to discover that our most private perceptions are universally felt.
- Why do we write? For the pleasure in the making, the re-imagining, the discovery of patterns that still come together as we grow older. For the uncovering of forms that echo our realities, that interrogate the established tradition, taking liberties, and gesturing—crudely, covertly, often unconsciously—toward a dozen alternate worlds.
- Becoming a writer involves discovering what you should write about and who your readers should be.
- Learn to rely on your own voice and to have faith in the value of your own experiences. There is an empty space on the bookshelf that only your voice and story can fill.
- Set out to discover what you may not have fully articulated even to yourself, bringing forth some fresh news from another country that enlarges your vision of the world.

~ 2 ~

MYTHS THAT KEEP YOU FROM WRITING

IT'S A CURIOUS FACT THAT WRITERS ARE OFTEN INEPT WHEN IT comes to discussing the subject of writing fiction. Alice Munro once said that telling someone how to write is like a juggler trying to explain how he keeps all those pie pans up in the air at the same time. Some writers have even described the act of writing as indescribable, indescribable being the one word that those who describe themselves as describers should never use. Quite a lot of writers can't tell you precisely what a short story is, and yet we purport to write them. There's something fairly audacious about this, you might say.

Ask a writer why he or she writes and there's likely to be a lot of shuffling of feet and looking the other way and almost no one in this non-heroic age is going to say, "I write because I have to."

And I have my writing.

"You have your writing!" friends say. A murmuring chorus: *But you have your writing, Reta.* No one is crude enough to suggest that my sorrow will eventually become material for my writing, but probably they think it.

—*Unless*

Writing is a mysterious process, and this vagueness about it makes it into a mystique. Writing is so various; it rises up from so many curious undetectable springs; it has so many contradictory intentions, and critical judgment swings so wildly that what is good writing in one decade is execrable in the next.

Like every mystique it has its set of shibboleths, its injunctions and freedoms, some of them true or untrue, helpful or harmful, and a good many constitute a systematic discouragement for the beginning writer. Let me mention a few of these myths.

Writing is performance. This statement has the impact of aphorism, and aphorism is something we must fix with a wary eye. It sounds good; therefore it must be true. Most writers will say that writing is a matter of groping your way to some kind of truth, an act of exploration. Joan Didion plainly said that she writes so that she can know what she is thinking, and V. S. Pritchett, a writer I particularly admire, said that he wrote so he could feel out the surface of what he is and where he lives. Notice the implicit modesty of these statements. And notice the moderate though not unintelligent voice. And notice how these assessments remove the burden some writers feel that they must make every word shimmer and every insight dazzle. Survey the whole field of fiction and you will see that pyrotechnics are only a small part of it. There is a great deal of moving people around, and listening to what they are saying.

Another injunction, a double one this time. All fiction is a form of autobiography. And the command: write about what you know.

This is a serious problem for a beginning writer since there's a good chance he undervalues what he knows and a good chance, too, that he doesn't want to risk exposure. Writers of course draw on their own experiences, but the fact is, few draw directly. As Alice Munro wrote in an essay entitled "What Is Real" in the magazine *Canadian Forum*, she requires for her fiction a portion of actual experience that acts as a kind of starter dough—I assume you're familiar with bread-baking terminology. To the starter can be added the subtle yeast of the imagined. John Irving, a writer I have grave reservations about, said in an essay that his writing comes out of the act of revising and redeeming actual experience. Pritchett goes all the way, saying a fiction writer's first duty is to become another person.

One of the most discouraging admonitions is this: don't begin to write until you have something to say. How often have you heard that one? Clearly everyone has something to say, whether he writes it down or not. You don't get to the age of six without knowing fear or intense happiness. You don't get to the age of twelve without having suffered. You don't arrive at eighteen without knowing what it is to love someone or, just as painful, not to love someone. Everyone has something to say; it may not be codified or arranged in the neat linear patterns of philosophy or the point of view of political commitment or as moral conviction, but the raw material is there, the "something" to write about.

Here's another one. If you want to be published you have to write for the market. I would suggest you begin writing without so much as glancing at the market. Unless you want to devote yourself to what's trendy: child custody stories one year, volcano disasters last year. Think instead of the stories you like to read, or better yet, the story you would like to read but can't find. And at this point, you might want to ask yourself if, in fact, you *like* reading short fiction. Do you prefer other forms? People in one short fiction class I taught told me they preferred long fiction but were afraid to tackle a novel. Short fiction was to be no more than an apprenticeship for the novel they hoped to write, and this is a premise I seriously question.

And we probably all know writers who, to earn a little money, have sat down to dash off a Harlequin romance or something similar. Nothing to it, they think, but the fact is they almost never succeed, for it is a fact that condescension shows in literature as well as in life. On the other hand, there's Barbara Cartland, the English writer of innumerable costume romances—the kind of book you may quite properly scorn. A few years ago, when she had to go into hospital for surgery, she looked around her house, her castle really, for some convalescent reading, and decided that the only thing that would really interest her were her own books. I think there's a lesson in this, that you must be committed to a certain kind of story in order to write it well.

> Romance novels … are able to fill their pages with dozens of strikingly beautiful women, and literary novels can permit a single heroine a rare beauty, one only. Light fiction, being closer to real life, knows better. Some imperfection must intervene, and usually this is in the nature of a slightly too long nose or a smaller than average chin. It is not necessary to award such disadvantages as giant hips or mannish shoulders and certainly not one eye larger than the other, although breasts may be on the small size or else more generous than normal.
>
> —*Unless*

There's a novel in everyone. You've heard this one. It's a myth that has suffered misinterpretation. There probably is material enough and more in every life, but does this mean that anyone, given the time, can write a novel? Time is what you sometimes hear people say they need. In fact, I have heard of one writer who got so tired of hearing people say, "I'd write a book if I had the time," that when he came to write his autobiography he titled it *I Had Time*. Time isn't enough. Skills of observation and skills of language (attention to rhythm, extension of vocabulary and distortion of syntax) are required. A feeling for structure. Stamina—for it takes an extraordinary effort to write even a bad novel or a completed short story.

Finishing has always seemed important to me. The end of a story is as important as the process. The feeling of completion, however imperfect, is what makes art, when we feel something being satisfied or reconciled or surrendered or earned. As Clark Blaise wrote, "an ending is after all the writer's last word on the subject and he'd better choose his words carefully."

You often hear that serious fiction needs to be underpinned by a myth structure, but work that is consciously manufactured around a myth tends to show all its nuts and bolts. Straining for seriousness almost invariably looks bogus while simple adherence to the truth does not. You may ask why I'm talking about truth when in fact we were talking—weren't we—about fiction. Fiction can be regarded as one of the purest forms of truth telling. Here is the truth that doesn't get into the biographies. Here are the unuttered thoughts of a human being laid bare for the first time. Even fantasy requires a truthful stretch of terrain in order not to look ludicrous. Myth, symbol, and, I would suggest, dream must be handled with extreme care. You've probably heard the story of the publisher who asked a writer if his book was done, and the author replied, "I'm all finished. I just have to go back and put the symbols in."

Another discouragement is this: all the good stories have been told. Or a variation of this: it's impossible to write a masterpiece and who wants to be a hack? It may be our literary critics who have put this burden on us. They talk for instance about something called unity of vision, as though anyone has ever possessed unity of vision or even wanted to. They talk about such and such a piece of work being flawed, as though there were ever an unflawed piece of work. They talk about major and minor work—and this is something to be careful of. Major, as Mary Gordon pointed out in an essay, often means Hemingway writing about boys in the wood; minor is Katherine Mansfield writing about women in the sitting room.

You also hear that writing is hard work, and with this I cannot disagree. There is an unfortunate myth that, once started, a story tends to write itself. Don't believe this. Writing is hard at the beginning of a story, hard in the middle, and hard at the end. There may be good days, a little momentum now and then, as though, as E. L. Doctorow said, "If you have one good day, you're punished for it the next."

In Brief . . .

Writing myths to ignore:

- All fiction is a form of autobiography.
- Write what you know.
- Don't begin to write until you have something to say.
- If you want to be published, you have to write for the market.
- There is a novel in everyone.
- Serious fiction needs to be underpinned by a myth structure.
- All the good stories have been told.
- It's impossible to write a masterpiece, as they've all been written.
- Once started a story tends to write itself.

Writing truths to embrace:

- Writing is hard work. Writing is hard at the beginning of a story, hard in the middle, and hard at the end.
- Straining for seriousness almost invariably looks bogus, while simple adherence to the truth does not.
- Pyrotechnics are only a small part of writing. There is a great deal of moving people around and listening to what they are saying.
- The end of a story is important. It is the feeling of completion, however imperfect, that makes art.

~ 3 ~

BOXCARS, COAT HANGERS
AND OTHER DEVICES

A NOVEL IS A WILD AND OVERFLOWING THING. ITS NARRATIVE, even when it is short and straightforward, includes a sort of encyclopedia of fact and notation and the gray spots in between, jumping from idea to idea, leaping continents and centuries and changes of mood. Novels—at least the novels I love to read—are mad-stuffed with people, events, emotional upheavals, and plateaus of despair. Their scenes dramatize arrivals, departures, births, marriages and murder, success and failure—the unsorted debris of existence, in fact, and yet their chaotic offerings are, when I look closely, attached to a finely stretched wire of authorly intention that reaches from the first page to the last.

How do novelists keep all this disorderly material on track? For years I fretted about the impossibility of the task, and kept putting off actually writing a novel. A novel, it seemed to me, was too big for someone who had scarcely been able to bring logic to a short story. Novels sprawled, or at least pretended to sprawl. Surely, characters or threads of thought got lost in the spreading chess game of prose, and no one could control it, least of all the inexperienced and fettered person sitting at the typewriter.

But I was getting close to forty, and, like many writers before me, I arrived at the now-or-never moment. Luckily for me, writing a master's thesis in my mid-thirties gave me a chip of courage; for the first time I had completed a *long* piece of writing and had discovered what should have been spectacularly self-evident: that long pieces of writing are made up of short pieces somehow sewn together.

Happily, my master's dissertation, about Susanna Moodie, a pioneer writer of the nineteenth century, contributed material for the novel that became *Small Ceremonies*. There were so many interesting footnotes I hadn't been able to incorporate, so much conjectural material that had been inadmissible in a scholarly document. And so, like my mother, who never threw out two tablespoons of leftover peas if she could help it, I decided to use up my research notes, to hand them over to a character I named Judith Gill, who, if the truth were known, was not all that different from myself, a woman nearing forty, a wife, a mother, a suburbanite—and someone who, like me, had an interest in history and in the idea of biography.

Because Judith Gill was part of an academic community, I arrived at the idea of using the academic year as a framework. My nine chapters were titled September, October, November, and so on, right through May. I didn't know where the novel was going, what its *substance* would be, but I found myself with a *structure* I could handle.

This structure felt to me like a series of similar-sized boxcars lined up on a track, nine of them. All I had to do was fill them up with "stuff," and I would have my novel. Every day when I sat down to write, I called up in my head the image of boxcars, much as we call up images on our computers. It kept me sane, the knowledge that my unruly, unsorted thoughts could be distributed along the timeline, each in its own container.

I've heard of writers who do complex outlines of their novels, but, in fact, I've never met one of these eager outliners. Writing for me is generated out of writing. I honestly don't know where I'm going. The ideas come as I push forward—some days there are too many swarming possibilities and other days not enough. But at least with that first novel, I had found a vehicle—my slowly loaded train—that allowed me to keep track of my novelistic bits and pieces.

My second novel, *The Box Garden*, was also built on the practical contrivance of a timeline, seven long chapters that more or less approximated the events of one week—approximate because I wanted to avoid being *too* schematic. I thought of these chapters as seven wire hangers on a coat rack. I didn't know what would be suspended from these hangers, but I knew their position and order. This novel was more compact in its events than the first, the temperature correspondingly higher, and more intense. The image of *my fictional week* was less important for the novel—which could have spilled into months or years—than it was for me, the writer; it gave me a disciplined structure that I could call on, depend on, and lean on. It made the maddening work of novel writing easier.

I don't know how other writers organize their material, but I suspect that each of us finds a way to keep control. I had a very clear image for my novel *Swann*, a book that broke free of many of the traditional narrative patterns I was accustomed to. Because of the point of view of the novel—four characters in search of a subject—I wanted the book to be built on four independent novellas with a concluding dramatization, each leaning just slightly on the others for coherence. This matrix swam into my mind very early in the writing. I was not absolutely wedded to it, but worked toward it, relying on it, and returning to it when I felt myself going off on wasteful tangents.

The original structure for *The Republic of Love* failed. My plan was to write a love story (a tricky business in these cynical times) by using a short notation from each day of a year, giving my book 365 related segments. This proved impossible, for I soon saw my novel swelling toward what looked like a thousand pages. I abandoned the plan and chose daily segments stretching from Easter to Christmas, a more manageable framework. The chapters of the novel alternate between the two lovers, Fay and Tom, and each chapter covers the events of one week, moving always forward on the timeline.

When I came to write *The Stone Diaries*, I again felt I needed a working image. I decided on a series of Chinese nesting boxes. I, the novelist, was constructing the big outside box; my heroine, Daisy Goodwill, struggling to understand her life, was making the next box, and the inside box was empty, a reminder to me of my original premise: that I was writing an account of a woman who was absent from her own existence. This organizing principle with its solid and easily retrievable image was not sketched out on paper and it certainly wasn't projected onto the reader. Instead, it served as my scaffold, my silent working orders and *aide-mémoire*.

These concrete structures—concrete in my mind, that is—have been tactically useful, but they have also forced me to open my mind to new ways of organizing fiction. We've all heard the rumour: the novel is dead. I don't believe this for a moment, but I do think certain traditional structures have lost their relevance. The old conflict/solution set-up feels too easy for me, too manipulative, and too often leading to what seems no more than a photo opportunity for people in crisis.

The structure of these kinds of novels could be diagrammed on a blackboard, a gently inclined line representing the rising action, then a sudden escalatory peak, followed by a steep plunge that demonstrates the dénouement, and then the resolution. I remember feeling quite worshipful in the presence of that ascending line. The novel as boxed kit, as scientific demonstration; and furthermore it was teachable.

It wasn't until I had been teaching literature for several years and passing on these inscribed truths to others that I started to lose faith. The diagram, which I had by then drawn on the blackboard perhaps fifty or sixty times, began one day to look like nothing so much as a bent spatula, and yet my students, hunched over the seminar table, were dutifully copying this absurd image into their notes.

Suddenly, I wasn't interested in the problem-solution story I had grown up with. The form seemed crafted out of the old quest myth in which obstacles were overcome and victories realized. None of this seemed applicable to the lives of women, nor to most of the men I knew, whose stories had more to do with the texture of daily life and the spirit of community than with personal battles, goals, mountaintops, and prizes.

I thought I understood something of a novel's architecture, the lovely slope of predicament, the tendrils of surface detail, the calculated curving upward into inevitability, yet allowing spells of incorrigibility, and then the ending, a corruption of cause and effect and the gathering together of all the characters into a framed operatic circle of consolation and ecstasy, backlit with fibre-optic gold, just for a moment on the second-to-last page, just for an atomic particle of time.

I had an idea for my novel, a seed, and nothing more.

—*Unless*

I had abandoned after my second novel the kind of people-in-crisis set-up that was the engine of so much realistic fiction. This meddling with form, though, was so gradual and tentative that I had scarcely been aware of it. Now I was. I felt emboldened enough to allow the fictions I was writing to fill up on the natural gas of the quotidian, and, without venturing into the inaccessible, to find new and possibly subversive structures.

More and more I trusted daily detail, wondering why domesticity, the shaggy beast that eats up fifty percent of our lives, had been shoved aside by fiction writers. Was it too dull, too insignificant, too flattened out, too obvious? I wanted wallpaper in my novels, cereal bowls, cupboards, cousins, buses, local elections, head colds, cramps, newspapers, and I abandoned Chekhov's dictum that if there is a rifle hanging over the fireplace, it must go off before the story ends. A rifle could hang over a fireplace for countless other reasons. For atmosphere, to give texture, to comment on the owner of the house, to ignite a scene with its presence, not its ammunition.

Out of her young, questioning self came the grave certainty that the family was the source of art, just as every novel is in a sense about the fate of a child. It might be argued that all literature is ultimately about family, the creation of structures—drama, poetry, fiction—that reflect our immediate and randomly assigned circle of others, what families do to us and how they can be reimagined or transcended.

—Jane Austen: A Life

The inclusion of domestic detail seemed much more to me than just an extra suitcase taken on board to use up my weight allowance. Diurnal surfaces could be observed by a fiction writer with a kind of deliberate squint that distorts but also sharpens beyond ordinary vision, bringing forward what might be called the subjunctive mode of one's self or others, a world of dreams, possibilities, and parallel realities.

In short, I wanted to write novels that were both tighter and looser. I wanted to create new structures that would give stability to the less stable material of my books and help me stay on course. And I wanted, then, to fill those structures with randomness, with side stories, surface details, potted histories, drifting thoughts—the whole raw material, in fact, of our lives. It meant taking a chance, looking around, tapping out words, shifting my sentences and paragraphs, getting the noises in my head onto paper, making something new.

In a sense, I use my structure as narrative bones, and partially to replace plot—which I more and more distrust. I'm comforted by something that Patrick White, the Australian novelist, once said: that he never worried about plot. What he wrote was life going on toward death. This is what interests me: the arc of a human life.

These are interesting times for a writer. The strands of reality that enter the newest of our novels are looser, more random and discursive. More altogether seems possible. The visual media, television and film have appropriated the old linear set-ups, leaving fiction, by default, the more interesting—to me—territory of the reflective consciousness, the inside of the head where most of our lives are lived.

In Brief . . .

- Remember that long pieces of writing are made up of short pieces sewn together.
- It helps to have a structure and an image of what those pieces are. Your structure serves as a scaffold, as silent working orders, and as an *aide-mémoire*.
- The structure could be
  - the months of a year
  - the days of a week
  - boxcars lined up on a track
  - wire hangers on a coat rack
  - linked novellas
  - alternating points of view
  - Chinese nesting boxes
- A structure should be approximate, instead of rigid, in order to avoid being too schematic.
- Traditionally, novels could be diagrammed as a gently inclined line representing the rising action, then a sudden escalatory peak, followed by a steep plunge that demonstrates the dénouement, and then the resolution. It is possible to find new and possibly subversive structures.

~ 4 ~

TO WRITE IS TO RAID

FICTION WRITERS, DOING THEIR PART TO PROMOTE THEIR BOOKS, welcome the chance to appear on a certain national network show. The host is genial and intelligent and, in fact, it seems he actually reads the books. Nevertheless the interviews almost always become a game of gentle cat-and-mouse in which the host attempts to link the work of fiction with the life of the writer, who is driven to cries of "No, no, this is fiction, I made it up."

"Well, yes," the host agrees, "but it must have really happened, if not to you then to someone else."

There is a curious opacity here, perhaps even a kind of honourable innocence that prefers to believe that people on the whole tell the truth and refrain from telling lies. This attitude, which seems to me to be very widespread, acknowledges the experience-plus-imagination recipe that makes fiction possible, but for some reason, devalues or distrusts the role of imagination.

Imagination, to be sure, is hard to talk about, this amorphous, transparent ether of the senses. We resort to metaphors, saying it is a kind of elementary wooden spoon with which we stir, blend, and generally rearrange life's offerings. Or we claim to lift it from the lint trap of our dreams or our unconscious. Or find it beneath a trapdoor labelled "What if—." Or describe it as a species of wistful daydreaming or the artful resculpting of actual experience to conform to a more satisfying aesthetic pattern. As I've mentioned, Alice Munro talked about "real" experience being a lump of starter dough. Everyone knows how little that small, damp, yeasty lump resembles the risen loaf with its lightness and fragrance, its imaginative dimensions and substantiality.

Russell Hoban, in a speech I heard a few seasons back, encouraged writers to *expand* our realities, to include in the realm of the real those not-so-rare moments of madness or transcendence. Audrey Thomas once declared in a radio interview that "everybody writes autobiography," but I wonder if she wasn't using the word autobiography as a filter that concentrates and refines the comprehended world and makes it legible to the individual consciousness. When Oonah McFee's first, and I think only, novel was published in 1977, she was asked if the book was autobiographical. "Well," she admitted, "there's at least an arm and a leg of me in it."

Just how much arm and leg gets into the writing varies enormously from one writer to another, but I don't believe there's a writer alive who hasn't struggled with the alchemy of re-imagined reality and the moral questions it poses. To write is to raid, the saying goes, although I suppose you might also say: to live is to raid, life being mainly a kind of cosmic lost-and-found bureau, or an everlasting borrowing and lending of personal and communal experiences.

Writer as thief, writer as scavenger—almost all writers feel the sting of such charges, even, I've noticed, beginning writers, or writers who have published nothing, or writers who are only just *thinking* about writing. The question generally arises early in a creative writing course: how can we deal honestly with the experiences of others without injuring them? How, too, can we deal with our own experiences without exposing ourselves unmercifully? My advice is always to write first and revise later (or *disguise* later as it were), since it's unlikely that a writer hobbled by the fear of giving offence is going to write at all. As my friend, the writer Sandy Duncan, says, there's no need to let the facts get in the way of the truth. The essential core of truth (that problematic word) need not necessarily be diminished if names are changed or if the short, fat bond salesman becomes the tall, thin lumberjack. In the same way River Heights can be renamed and moved to Nova Scotia if you like, or even to Mars or Baloneyland. The fictional variables can be moved forward or backward in time, or else the timeline can be fractured or even smudged. (By the way, an astute interviewer once fixed me with a steady eye and demanded to know why the women in my novels were invariably tall and large-boned, with heads of thick, dark, curly hair.)

> I like to sketch in a few friends, in the hope they will provide a
> release from a profound novelistic isolation that might otherwise
> ring hollow and smell suspicious.
>
> —*Unless*

I would defend the right of writers to use *any* experience they choose in their fiction, but I have come to think that it is more charitable, kinder that is, to refrain from embarrassing others or borrowing their stories without permission or else dramatic revision, or especially, redemption. Like everyone else, writers need to sleep easily at night. "I don't write about my family members or friends," says novelist Barbara Kingsolver, "because I want them to remain family members and friends."

But beyond the ethical questions of exploitation, beyond the simple respect for the privacy of others, is the work itself, and I am convinced that the increased weight of the imaginative element contributes to the aesthetic power of a piece of writing. Colouring outside the lines may be harder to accomplish, but can yield more in the end than simple follow-the-dot transference. (Yes, I do recognize this as a botched metaphor, but I give myself permission to use it.)

On the other hand, I think we owe our work the texture and taste of the apprehended world, and it seems to me ungenerous to withhold those few insights we may have gathered along the way. Kennedy Fraser, in an essay on Virginia Woolf, confesses that she once suffered a time in her life that was so painful that reading about the lives of other women was the only thing that comforted her. She claims she was slightly ashamed of this, pretending to her friends that she was reading the novels and the poetry of these women. But in fact it was their lives that supported her.

"I needed," she says, "all that murmured chorus, this continuum of true-life stories, to pull me through. They were like mothers and sisters to me, these literary women, many of them already dead; more than my own family, they seemed to stretch out a hand." I have seen this passage from Kennedy Fraser's essay quoted a dozen times, and can only guess that it summons up the writer-reader relationship that so many of us know and are indebted to.

In particular, Fraser says, the brave autobiographical writings of Virginia Woolf answered her, as they also helped heal Woolf's own pain. In her fifties, shortly before she died, Virginia Woolf set down the history of child abuse she had suffered, and wrote that "By putting it into words...I make it whole; this wholeness means that it has lost its power to hurt me."

"Honest, personal writing," Fraser concludes in her essay, "is a great service rendered the living by the dead." What we need to establish, perhaps, is a new form, a form that invites the personal without risk to the self or to others and one that incorporates the author's voice without giving way to self-indulgence. One thinks of diaries or certain forms of memoirs or docu-fiction, forms that attempt to place the self in time.

Think of the loss to history if we fail to record the full and authentic lives of people, their private lives, their domestic lives. When Canadian writer Peter Ward began working on his book *Courtship, Love, and Marriage in Nineteenth-Century English Canada*, he came, he says, "head-on into the frustration shared by all who want to know what the silent Canadians of the past thought and felt. The evidence of personal experience and feelings, of private conduct and personal relationships, is at best fragmentary." The "Maps and Chaps" recording of history, as it is sometimes called, has carried forward only the sketchiest outline of society. It is no wonder that novelist Margaret Drabble has been called a true chronicler of the late twentieth century; her novels hold the randomness of felt lives, the diurnal rub and drub of existence as it is experienced by at least a segment of our population. The eccentric but captivating fictions of Nicholson Baker rather bravely, I think, risk triviality in order to record what we all experience but hesitate to enter on the page: the sensation of a shoelace breaking loose in the hand, for instance, or the precise colour and muscular flicker of a baby's eyelid. The sensations, recordings and reorderings of these writers, and others like them, add up to more than the sum of their small parts.

This kind of writing takes time. You have to pay attention. You have to have the patience to move the words around until they are both precise and allusive. I believe it is worth the effort. You can think of such fictions as entries on a ledger that push past print into an expanded reading of our world in all its intricacies and mysteries.

In Brief . . .

- To write is to raid, the saying goes. Writing is like life: a kind of cosmic lost-and-found bureau, an everlasting borrowing and lending of personal and communal experiences.
- How to avoid harming or wounding others? Write first, and revise (or disguise) later. If you're hobbled by the fear of giving offence, you're unlikely to write at all.
- Refrain from embarrassing others or borrowing their stories without permission. Like everyone else, writers need to sleep easily at night.
- You have to pay attention and have the patience to move the words around until they are both precise and allusive.

~ 5 ~

BE A LITTLE CRAZY; ASTONISH ME

CAN YOU REALLY TEACH PEOPLE TO WRITE? I MIGHT POSE A PAR-allel question: do we really teach people to be philosophers or mathematicians? Don't we, instead, hand over to our budding philosophers or mathematicians a few basic tools that permit them to self-evolve?

Perhaps what we really mean when we say we can't teach writing is that we can't teach someone to be Virginia Woolf. On the other hand, a number of our most accomplished writers were, early in their lives, enrolled in writing courses: Eugene O'Neill, Tennessee Williams, Arthur Miller, Wallace Stegner, and Flannery O'Connor, to name a few.

Ah, but writing is God-given, it's often said, the implication being that the writer is also God-protected and superhuman, an uncomfortable assumption for most of us these days. Those who reject the God-given thesis sometimes believe that Bohemia is the place to learn to write. But Bohemia, that mythical realm—meaning freedom from compromise and convention, an excited, open state of mind, a portable set of liberties that fertilize the ground from which writers spring—has not much flourished in North America.

Writers are romantically believed to be seekers of solitude, but in fact they have historically gathered around centres of power. Today the university has become one of those power centres, delivering encouragement in the shape of course offerings and informed tutoring. A centre of learning, it can be argued, is an appropriate venue for the teaching of writing since it also possesses libraries, bookstores, accommodation, staff, classrooms—and, most important, people who know how to write and who are willing to share their knowledge and intuition with those who are learning. Haven't writers always, in fact, functioned this way—teaching, coaching, mentoring, advising, editing and influencing other writers—in garrets or coffee houses or the courts of kings or in country houses, through correspondence, or by the simple dissemination of their books? The place of interaction has shifted; a slight and gradual formalization has occurred, but the process is not radically different from what it's always been.

Early writing programs, perhaps in order to defend their legitimacy in the university, were often rather traditionally organized, using textbooks and assigning letter grades for weekly assignments. They were, in fact, institutions that ran on the gas of criticism rather than creativity. Gradually the workshop evolved, becoming the cornerstone of most creative writing programs, and there are some who believe that this manner of teaching has influenced the way learning has come to be shared in other enlightened (that is, non-hierarchical) disciplines. Basically, workshopping in creative writing programs means that the work of students is read and critiqued by members of the class and by the writer/teacher who acts as a sort of group leader. Ideally students are drawn out, cajoled, persuaded, questioned, nudged, niggled and encouraged to make a new and personal set of criteria, rather than fed a critical line or one way to approach creating fiction.

If this methodology sounds vaguely, nostalgically familiar, it may be because it gestures toward the methodology of the medieval or even classical university. Obviously students are not taught how to be original, but they are made aware of non-originality and they are exposed, though not perhaps systematically, to certain skills involved in writing: setting up a scene and furnishing it, situating a narrative in time and space, controlling the flow of information, creating a mood, deciding who is telling the story and why.

In 1973, all the teachers of creative writing in colleges and universities in the United States were invited to a conference in Washington, D.C., hosted by the Library of Congress. Five hundred writers/teachers attended, among them such luminaries as John Barth, Wallace Stegner, John Ciardi and Ralph Ellison. The animated discussions between the participants brought to light some disturbing revelations. Only about one percent of creative writing students became writers. Ninety-nine percent of students of the day were "lured by the glamour of the profession or the desire for money and fame." (I can only suppose that these numbers were arrived at anecdotally rather than statistically.)

Three other discoveries came out of the meeting. 1. No one knows how to teach writing. 2. In particular, no one knows how to teach the talented. And 3. The talentless can be taught only a little.

It might be thought that these dismal conclusions would spell the end of creative writing teaching in America. Exactly the opposite occurred. Courses in creative writing proliferated, writer-in-residence programs were established in all corners of the country, writers' retreats (often with a writer/teacher available) flourished, and degree-granting writing programs grew in number and in power, and their presence was more and more seen as a sign of prestige for their mother institutions.

Creative writing courses are often the only place in our society where writers can come together. They are our salons, our "left banks," our wine bars, the laboratories of our literature. Creative writing classes give to students of literature a glimpse of the way in which literature is made, how difficult it is and how fragile and fleeting the creative impulse is. A certain sharpening of critical ability occurs in these classes, at least some of it self-directed. In addition, writing courses seize upon that compulsion most young people have to write a poem or story, to say something in words that are entirely their own. A social function is served, too, I think. These classes are, after all, small and intense, and deal frequently with highly personal material. A student once told me that reading his own writing to a class was like standing up and taking off all his clothes. Certain standards of kindness and trust must be established and adhered to. I think many of these social transactions are useful, more useful in the long run perhaps than aesthetic transactions.

At the time my novel about Judith Gill was published (*Small Ceremonies*, 1976), I had had no experience at all with creative writing classes, either as student or teacher, and in my "creative" description of such a class *in Small Ceremonies* I turned out to be partly right and partly wrong. I was right—and I can only suppose that I had picked up a certain amount of random information by a kind of osmosis—about the general informality of such classes—the seventies were, after all, the days of encounter groups, of such experiments as the human potential movement. I was right about there being a wide variation in students' backgrounds and ages, right on the whole about the size of classes—they do vary from ten to twenty—right about those little class exercises, and right, too, about the rather nervously offered and vaguely worded student criticism. But I was wrong about student boldness, the desire to shock, and student willingness to abandon themselves in their writing and to their classmates. Creative writing students are often painfully guarded; it is one of the great problems of teaching. And I was wrong about student commitment to philosophical or political causes. It is the self that chiefly interests them, the lonely self, the misunderstood self, and this produces a kind of writing that is often claustrophobic and, worse, bewilderingly private. Finally, I was wrong to believe that students exhaust themselves in their initial cathartic explosions. In fact, it takes several weeks to establish an atmosphere of trust in a class, and it is only then that creative and critical skills begin to grow.

I try to establish an atmosphere of creativity, not correction, and I begin each new class by introducing myself, asking students to use my first name, Carol, since I intend to use their first names. Sitting around a seminar table, it seems to me, demands the informality of first names, although I have no idea whether other writer/teachers feel comfortable with this particular form of familiarity. I explain to my newly registered class, as undramatically as I can, that I am a writer, and I list briefly what I have written. I outline in about a hundred words or less what I consider writing to be about, and for and of, and then I make a point never to refer again to my own work or, directly, to my own writerly views. When teaching, I insist on setting a distance from my own work because I am wary of imposing my ideas and my methodology on developing writers who are, as you might imagine, almost dangerously open to suggestion.

(I recall teaching a short fiction class at the University of British Columbia in which the previous instructor had decreed that writing in the first person was masturbatory and therefore indecent—it took me a full year to restore confidence in the first person voice.) Each writer evolves a method of writing or an approach to writing that is personally productive and engaging and rewarding. I write 500 words a day, but I am not at all anxious to press this limit on eighteen-year-old students or even on forty-year-old students. I write every day, whether or not I am ignited by the force of what some call the fire of inspiration, but I would not want to suggest to others that their thirty-six-hour or sixty-four-hour flights of inspired intemperance are wasteful and self-indulgent because I am not at all sure they are.

I make it a point to declare to the class at our first meeting that everything—that is, all material—is open to scrutiny except that which is pornographic or sexist—and occasionally we disagree as a class about the limits of these two reservations. What constitutes sexist writing? Why is a long, voluptuous and explicit sex scene acceptable and an off-hand reference to a hateful, hairy-legged woman not? This question came up in my class once and I'm not sure it was satisfactorily resolved.

I always ask my students at the first class to introduce themselves and to reveal why they have registered for the course. Only very occasionally does a student say: "I want to become a great writer." Generally they respond by saying modestly: "Because I want to learn to sharpen my images, or write better dialogue, or test my material on an interested audience." Once a woman replied that she wanted to discover what a story was. Good luck, I said to myself, since I've never been able to frame a satisfactory definition myself.

I ask them to write down what they consider to be the hardest thing about writing, and over the years I've collected such responses as: Knowing how to begin. Knowing when I've reached the end. Getting the thoughts in my head onto paper. Finding time. Learning to concentrate. Finding my own voice. Avoiding libel and/or injury to others—chiefly mothers. (Mothers, I've found, take a hard knock in creative writing courses.)

Believing students should write the stories they would like to read, I brace myself and ask new students what they read. Some confess to reading nothing but texts for their other classes. Almost all of them read Stephen King and Sidney Sheldon; younger students are wrapped up with Kurt Vonnegut; one or two will have read Margaret Atwood, usually for a class. A few have read Alice Munro and Anne Tyler. Most say they prefer to read novels, but they want to write short stories. Why? Because the size of the novel frightens them.

I begin each three-hour class with a short discussion of some aspect of writing—tension, tone, voice, and so on. Then we do an in-class writing exercise. Over the years I've collected certain exercises that work, at least most of the time. I might for instance pass around a photograph of a human hand, and ask them to write for six minutes, using the voice of the owner of the hand. I then give them two or three minutes to edit their material, and then we go around the table reading what we've written. Or I might give them a single word, the word "pink," for instance, and ask them to run with it in any direction they choose. These exercises do a number of things, showing the students how variable responses can be and how readily available the source of creativity is. Often I repeat an exercise and say, "Take it further at this time." It's as though they need someone to say: Be a little crazy. Astonish me.

Part of the class will be spent on a reading of the weekly assignment. A typical assignment might be: write a paragraph describing a room without using any adjectives. I ask the students to provide copies of their work for the class. We keep the critiques of these exercises short, bearing in mind that they are exercises, attempts, experiments, and not finished work.

Every student declares a major project within the first month. I ask for a short story of no less than fifteen pages; a short play, about twenty-five pages; or a group of poems, about fifteen pages. We workshop two of these projects a week, discussing them in detail, offering oral and also written comments.

A very great improvement in writing is seen within weeks, particularly after the problems of clichés and sentimentality are identified. An understanding of point of view brings further improvement. But then I notice a slowing down. It is possible, it seems, to teach people how to write better, but impossible to get them to have better *ideas*. What writers need is to learn to notice things, to recognize a story when they see it and to trust their impulses. A creative writing teacher can to a certain extent give permission. A teacher can also say: You will have to write 300 words by next Wednesday, and this kind of deadline is a spur to a student who has been meaning to get around to writing for twenty years. Creative writing classes also provide an opportunity to try out material on an audience, although in fact that audience is often poorly equipped in terms of a critical vocabulary and with the kind of courage it takes to deal vigorously and honestly with the work of peers.

Marking is a special problem, and some advocate that pass/fail marks would be more appropriate. I base marks on attendance, participation, commitment to writing and to the class, and on improvement. This last is highly subjective, as you can imagine.

> To write is to be self-conscious, as Jane Austen certainly knew. What flows onto paper is more daring or more covert than a writer's own voice, or more exaggerated or effaced.
>
> —*Jane Austen: A Life*

Writing classes tend for some reason to be less homogeneous than other university classes, and so new and unexpected accommodations must be reached. How will an eighteen-year-old youth, fresh from a suburban high school, find a measure of commonality with a fifty-year-old man who has been fired from his engineering job, who is freshly divorced, who is a single father, who has recently been hospitalized for a nervous breakdown? (This sounds like a collision out of a soap opera, but it nevertheless occurred in a course I once taught.) Will a twenty-year-old woman, a lover of Stephen King and a fundamentalist Christian, be able to comprehend an ironic, cryptic, emotionally charged short story written by a sixty-year-old woman, the wife of a psychology professor, a woman who has wanted to write for thirty years but felt blocked before writing a single word? Will a young man who has written a gothic horror story in which the hero dies by being flushed down the toilet have anything to say to a young woman who has produced a dozen short exquisite prose pieces about the fantasy, the seduction, the necessity—so she says—of her own projected suicide?

The human transactions that take place in writing class are enormously useful in the long run, perhaps more useful than the aesthetic transactions.

It had always seemed something of a miracle to him that poetry *did* occasionally speak. Even when it didn't he felt himself grow reverent before the quaint, queer magnitude of the poet's intent. When he thought of the revolution of planets, the emergence of species, the balance of mathematics, he could not see that any of these was more amazing than the impertinent human wish to reach into the sea of common language and extract from it the rich dark beautiful words that could be arranged in such a way that the unsayable might be said. Poetry was the prism that refracted all of life. It was Jimroy's belief that the best and worst of human experiences were frozen inside these wondrous little toys called poems.

—*Swann*

Writing Assignments

I. Write a poem, incorporating a phrase from a poet you love. Ask yourself:

    a. Does it have musicality?

    b. Is it concrete, not just a flying package of feelings?

    c. Does it say what you really mean, or are you trying to be poetic?

    d. Are all the words as effective as possible? For any weak word, get a thesaurus and find a better one.

    e. Who do you imagine reading or hearing it?

    f. Is this person going to understand it?

    g. Are you being overly sentimental or manipulating the reader?

h. Can you shout this poem out loud without
   sounding ridiculous and without getting your tongue
   in a knot?

i. Does your poem have an idea of some kind? It should be
   about something.

2. Discuss: Can a poem be bad?

3. Write a poem, short story or play of approximately two
   pages in which a change of direction is announced, i.e., set
   something up and then turn it.

4. Write *one good sentence.* Not pretty, not full of metaphor.
   A good, pure, solid slug of a sentence.

5. What is something you have always wanted to write but
   never have?

6. Write a sentence about a Matisse painting.

7. Write a sentence about a squash.

8. Write a poem in the same rhythm as the Lord's Prayer, but use
   your own words.

9. Write 250 words in the form of a complete stretch of dialogue
   or prose poem that includes a needle, a ticket stub and a glass
   of milk.

10. Look at a photograph of a hand and write about the specific
    talents and experiences the owner of the hand has.

11. Look at a headshot of a man in a suit and write about
    who he is.

12. Write 250 words about one person giving a gift that is refused.

13. Write something in which the world is a blank slate,
    without history.

14. Look at or imagine an antique postcard with this written
    on the back: "I am going to get one like this for Aunt Etta.

You want to be sure the door is locked when you go to bed. Lillian." Bounce off the postcard message and write one sharply focused page.

15. Translate the following passage creatively. Look at the shapes of words. This is an exercise in spontaneity and boldness of attack.

> *Nie wurden flue hawkender est ålt dek bitten. Duo wingen bresse plus tet plus pies groupen "English." Michélene floten sur el duro puis la reve. Sel cran, "Nie, nie, nie." Loes frags cran lottisment plus strangement. Ottrest ållo plus quiété. Calssico classico, clangenhart classico. "Hush, hushen," lo cran. Plasticity dur colunber est trister quan brite-meet. Injery? Broden? Lo sense, "Les toiles bran son ciecle des Bruxelles, plus la west ciecle." Blesse plus centres, janais outframe. Argent spile otre nos pies, plus los crans. Yaf nie Holland, yaf nie Belge. Los brancher torn plus crassa. Lo flue est blue, dek plus bitten. Silénćo, silénćo. Warden para chaumiére.*

~ 6 ~

WHAT YOU USE AND WHAT YOU PROTECT

A WRITER OF A FIRST NOVEL FOUND HERSELF DEEPLY INJURED BY the few and grudging reviews she received, but she was affected even more by something else: how much of herself, her life, her experience she had given away in her book—wasted, she called it, used up. Her experience was her *capital*, as she loved to say, and how much experience was left to her for the next time around?

How often can you write away the well of yourself? I am going to speak here about a writing life and how the parts of the self seep into a writer's fiction, and spill out, flowing into literary biography.

Let me suggest to you that when a writer sits down to write, there are two people at the keyboard, not one. There is the performer, the creator, the storyteller. And seated next to her, or perhaps crouched inside her, is the source—that being who has laid down a bedrock of thought, of experience, or perhaps of bewilderment and inexperience, and she is now eager to write out of the sum or distillation of that reserve, to *name* what Philip Larkin once called "the million-petaled flower of being." For no matter how much objective research a fiction writer does, no matter which realms of the imagination are attempted, there is inevitably a trace or a teaspoon or an arm or a leg of herself in what she writes. This, in fact, is what is so frightening about writing fiction: what we inadvertently reveal, the degree to which we expose ourselves.

One critic wrote that there was a series of detached and ineffectual fathers appearing in Carol Shields' fiction. Really? Can this be true? Well yes, on examination, those fathers do seem to pop up rather often. I am cagey about this confession; I need to think more about it. What can it mean and where does it come from? Another example: The literary editor of *Le Droit* interviewed me in Paris after having read with extreme care everything I'd written. I had never met before or since such a well-prepared journalist. And she had discovered something I hadn't known: "Il n'y a pas d'animaux dans vos livres," she charged. "There are no animals in your books." I was astonished, but yes, I agreed, on reflection, that she was quite correct, although there is a passing reference to a parrot in a 1985 short story and another to a fish—but then it is a *painting* of a fish that is mentioned and not the creaturely fish itself. Distant fathers, an absence of animals—what do these unintentional gaps signify, if anything?

We scatter our texts with unwitting clues to who we are and what consumes us. Not long ago, I received a letter from a dental hygienist in North Carolina, a woman who writes a monthly column for the American Society of Dental Hygienists newsletter. "You have a great many references in all your books," she wrote, "to teeth," and she then supplied me with a long list of page references. What precisely was my relationship to teeth, she wanted to know. Well!? Teeth are part of life, I ventured in reply. We have an emotional *investment* in our teeth—but even to me this seemed not quite answer enough. *Am* I just a little obsessed with chewing and grinding? Is my unconscious view of the world dental-driven?

We are as writers responsible—or are we?—for our offered up passions and for our buried themes, even those buried out of sight of our own eyes, even that which we have not articulated to ourselves.

My early novels all included teenaged children—not at the centre of the story, perhaps, but caught *somewhere* in the web of the narrative. But a 1987 novel, titled *Swann*, had, I realized when I read the proofs, no children at all. By 1993, children had returned to my pages, and even I could figure out what that meant.

Writing a novel set in Winnipeg, I was faithful to the sense of Winnipeg as I saw it, but carefully skewed the spellings of some of the street names and institutions, a subliminal message to the reader that the Winnipeg I was writing about was a city dressed in its fictional robes, not quite the real thing. This seemed important, perhaps for my own protection against error or perhaps to assert and protect the freedom fiction writers are accorded.

And early on, while I'd decided not to write about my friends and family, I realized that even writing about acquaintances can be tricky. In the midst of writing my first novel, for instance, I was out shopping one day and ran into an acquaintance, a woman of about my own age. She, too, had been shopping, and she opened her shopping bag to show me a beautiful sea-green nightgown she'd bought. "And now," she said, "I must be on my way. I'm trying to find some candles to match my nightgown." "Really," I said, and she must have seen my jaw drop because she said, "Oh, I have candles to match all my nightgowns."

I couldn't resist preserving this moment. This little anecdote found its way into my text, a delectable throwaway—but when I read the proofs, I really did decide to throw it away, reasoning that she was quite likely to read my novel, and that she might recognize herself, being probably the only woman in the Western hemisphere or even in the world who carried bedroom coordination to this degree.

We're told that certain people feel their soul is appropriated when their photograph is taken, and this strikes me as being at least partly reasonable. There is no one, even in the cause of Great Literature, upper case letters, who wants to be ridiculed, injured, or even embarrassed; there is no one who wants even to feel overly observed and commented upon, though I do defend to the death those writers who live closer to the autobiographical bone than I've chosen to do and who write about their own ex-husbands, beastly mothers and ungrateful children.

> For every writer the degree of required social involvement or
> distance must be differently gauged, but novelists who take refuge
> in isolated log cabins tend to be a romantic minority, or perhaps
> even a myth. Most novelists, knowing that ongoing work is fed by
> ongoing life, prize their telephones, their correspondence, and
> their daily rubbing up against family and friends.
>
> —*Jane Austen: A Life*

However, using the great world about me and the droplets that fall from it is something else. This is the source of at least half a fiction writer's material. A friend of mine who suffers from frequent laryngitis told me her husband claims her throat is her Achilles heel, a witticism that appealed to me, and I asked her if I could use it—yes, she said, she expected me to use it. She had told it to me *because she knew* it would appeal to me.

I've heard writers say that their friends wouldn't recognize themselves if they apprehended their image in the pages of a novel. Writerly paint would have blurred the outlines; writerly invention would have added enough ornamentation to conceal the true identity.

But readers are not so easily fooled as this, especially readers who have collided with novelists or even befriended them. They know they are in danger the minute they are admitted to a writer's life, and they read the published text with a magnifying lens in hand.

Could that be me, that fool dribbling coffee down his shirtfront and babbling about the tyranny of life in the suburbs, about the betrayal of love? Yes, of course it's me.

During the twenty or so years I taught classes in creative writing, I never once encountered a student who didn't worry, at some level, that a friend or family member was going to be violated, punished or crucified in a piece of writing. (Mothers take an exceptionally heavy rap with younger students.) This fear persisted even among students whose work would stand scarcely any chance of ever being published. The concern was real, and often it afflicted young writers with classic writer's block before they'd written so much as a single word.

I always urged them to say what they had to say anyway, unshackled by any thought of personal response. They could revise afterward, I said, burying the real person by altering gender, race, the time frame, the geographical context. The choices were limitless. Write bravely, truly; revise with discretion, tact. This is easy enough to say, but I have come to understand exactly how difficult it is in the end to make the small and necessary sacrifices once words are committed to paper. There are times when changing even a name feels like a hideous compromise.

Like most writers, I have become an attentive eavesdropper. A whole short story slid into view one day when I found myself sitting behind two divinity students on a bus and overhearing a discussion about why Lot's wife was turned to salt when she disobediently looked back. The use of public transportation, I should say, can be extremely profitable to fiction writers, who are always looking to restock their supplies. And so are such public places as elevators or restaurants. Seated one day at an outdoor café, I found myself caught between two discussions, a conversational cross-draft if you like. At one table, two women were discussing a highly dramatic love affair one of them was having, and at the other table were two businessmen, suits, haircuts, the look of seriousness. The older man turned to the younger and said, boomingly, "We'll cross that bridge when we get to the bottom of the barrel."

My favourite eavesdrop of all time, and one I was able to use eventually in a book, occurred at Niagara Falls, where I stood on a summer's day not far from a group of tourists from Brooklyn, one of whom turned to his friends and said, loudly, clearly, as he gazed out at the beauty of the falls, "Jeez, it makes you thoisty, don't it, lookin' at all dat watah."

Years ago, on a soft spring evening, I went for a walk and observed a young man sitting on a folding chair on his front lawn. He had an ironing board in front of him, and on the ironing board a portable typewriter, and he was typing with such speed, such verve, such happiness—never looking up, of course—that I knew as he flung the carriage back that he was in the midst of an inspired creative act. "What are you writing?" I longed to call out, but didn't.

We live after all in a society that forbids the intimate interrogating of strangers. Inquisitive people are discouraged and certainly disparaged. Journalists and biographers may be given special privileges, allowed to ask their Nosy Parker questions, but the rest of us are forced to deal imaginatively with the great gaps.

For novelists this means observing, listening at the keyhole as well as peering into it, gently probing, but in the end risking ourselves and our small truths, *guessing* at the way other people live and think, hoping to get it right at least part of the time.

I long ago understood that the silences our society imposes give to the novelist a freshness of opportunity, a way to bring spaciousness and art into the smallest, most ordinary lives. Even so, I suffer as many writers do from a scavenger's guilt, and always experience a desire to include on the title page of my books some small message of acknowledgement: "Forgive me." Or "I'm sorry."

Notes for Novel

Tweedy man on bus, no change, leaps off

beautiful girl at concert, husband observes her legs, keeps dropping program

children in park, sailboat, mother yells (warbles) "Damn you David. You're getting your knees dirty."

letter to editor about how to carry cello case in a mini-car. Reply from bass player

West Indians queue for mail. Fat white woman (rollers) cigarette in mouth, "what they need is ticket home."

story in paper about woman who has baby and doesn't know she's preg. Husband comes home from work to find himself a father. Dramatize.

leader of labour party dies tragically, scramble for power. wife publishes memoirs.

hotel bath. each person rationed to one inch of hot water. Hilarious landlady.

Lord renounces title so he can run for House of Commons, boyhood dream and all that.

—*Small Ceremonies*

I'm sometimes asked what it was like to be a novelist living in the city of Winnipeg, and beneath this question, I believe I hear a certain floating skepticism—how can works of the imagination be written if there are no magnificent mountains to provide inspiration, if there is no pounding surf to carry one away, no fragrance and persistence of tropical foliage? The city where I live *does* have its own smells and landscape and music, but, despite what my friend Eleanor Wachtel reminds us—that *geography is destiny*—none of this matters much since writers perform their tasks in small rooms on the whole with the door closed. Their scenery is the interior life with its collection of images, discoveries, scenes, observations, dreams—that whole unwieldy cotton sack of material we refer to as memory.

What is produced in the shut room by way of the lint of memory is often fiction, not memoir. Yet even memoir is more than the pinning down of actual experience. The critic Brigitte Frase calls the memoir "an artful dodger, slip-sliding though the facts of autobiography and journalism into the techniques of fiction. It is," she says, "the most rhetorically dramatic of forms, in the way it shines full-glare lights on some episodes, while others are left in haunting, suggestive shadows…dealing out revenge, wallowing in showy humilities."

We live in an anti-romantic age, and so we are uncomfortable with the idea that writers do not choose their work out of a combination of interest and ability but are somehow "chosen." Also rejected by most is the narcissistic idea of the writer as filter through whose fine mesh God speaks, or else nations or history or the channelled voices of greatness. The writer, in fact, is a person with a self as slippery as your own and as prey to amnesia or distortion, as fearful of death as you, and, like you, always fighting against a sense of lowered consequence. Writers are also beings in need of clean clothes, heat, a fairly comfortable chair and good lighting. Their writerly fidgets, doubts, skin rashes, and aching teeth—those teeth again—spill directly into the false efforts and random successes of their writing.

This is why it seems strange to reflect on the force of the New Criticism, sometimes called the Cambridge Movement, which was the prevailing literary theory of the late thirties, forties and early fifties, the time that I first encountered literature in its formal shape. The New Criticism eschewed any interest in the writer behind the writing, the separate self with a personal history who sewed together the fabric of language and narrative.

A life is full of isolated events, but these events, if they are to form a coherent narrative, require odd bits of language to cement them together, little chips of grammar (mostly adverbs or prepositions) that are hard to define, since they are abstractions of location or relative position, words like *therefore, else, other, also, thereof, theretofore, instead, otherwise, despite, already,* and *not yet.*

—*Unless*

The New Critics worked by means of close textual analysis, considering the text as the final—in fact, the only—authority. They distrusted the lights and shadows of the writer's life and experience, the writer's methods and attitudes or, in fact, anything that did not actually appear within the margins of the finished page. I remember being quite worshipful about the New Criticism; believing absolutely in this clean and pure form of literary response, I stole only *a few* guilty glances at the author photo on the back cover. Indeed, author photos shrivelled in size during this period and sometimes disappeared. It was as though all the writers of the world belonged to the same scout troop and drew from a shared pool of images and style so that their texts—that crisp and useful word—could go out into the world on their own sturdy, anonymous, boy-scout legs.

By the fifties, the purity of this belief had become muddied. Readers felt obscurely cheated; writers felt depersonalized. The whole set-up was too ivory-toned, too difficult to apply evenly, and too damaging to the contract between writer and reader.

It was Jean-Paul Sartre, I think, who said, "To read a book is to write it." This seems to me a rather profound observation, since the reader of a text does, in fact, travel the same hills and valleys of thought as the writer, uncovering along with the writer the same revelations, leading to somewhat similar though never perfectly congruent emotional leaps and thrusts.

The writer-reader connection *must be* one of the most intimate in human experience, the voice of the writer going not onto a large shared public screen, but directly, privately, leaving the shut room and entering the single consciousness of the reader who makes the cognitive shift inside a *singular* and *particular* brain, translating symbol to meaning and thereby becoming part of the creative process. The reader *knows* the writer, not just the written work. St. Augustine believed the act of reading to be a conversation with the absent, and the word conversation is interesting here, since reading in Augustine's time meant mainly reading out loud (although St. Augustine himself was said to have read silently).

Some writers resent the public's need to know who they are. I have a friend who, when she goes on book tours, wants to shout out crossly into the audience, "You read the book, now here's the body." She doesn't want to share her secrets, to betray where she gets her ideas or admit to certain influences, and she certainly doesn't want to be asked whether she writes with a computer or a pen, or what she eats for breakfast.

But the fact is, those who have chosen a writing life have already surrendered a portion of their DNA. There are all those clues in their work, all those revealing gaps that I spoke of earlier, *all those teeth,* and there is the implicit contract they have formed with their reader. They may choose to shroud their lives in privacy—think of J. D. Salinger, of Thomas Pynchon, of Anne Tyler, Don DeLillo— but autobiography comes spilling through the work itself. Attitude. Distance. Geography. Gender. Intellect. Education. The ability to embrace the real or create the "other." Risk. Love. Damage. Vision.

All these draw an outline of the self-reflective human consciousness that writes a book into being and places that book in the reader's hands.

> Nevertheless, publication meant having a public self after a life
> that had been austerely private. Her scale of values, her opinions
> were now being read by a wide public, and not just received by the
> family circle. The two selves, public and private, were in danger of
> flying apart, but her correspondence shows her efforts to hang on
> to all that was familiar while enjoying the titillation of celebrity.
> —*Jane Austen: A Life*

Some of you may have had an opportunity to look at a facsimile of a manuscript by Marcel Proust. I like to show a page or two of Proust's work to my classes as an example of a text that is rethought, reworked and enlarged by a mind that is electric with thought and hard at work, generous in its energy and patient with the demand for precision. Only the most patient literary sleuth can make out Proust's manuscript pages, they are so covered with changes, additions, explications, refinements, emendations, scribbles in the margin, the better phrase, the more exact word. This has to tell us something about the writer-reader contract, and in fact it does.

> I work on my sonnets at a small keyhole desk in a corner of our
> blue-and-gray bedroom. I actually work with real paper, lined
> paper from a thick tablet, and a ballpoint pen, with a great many
> crossings-out and dozens of arrows and question marks and
> sometimes such marginal scribblings as "No!" or "saccharine" or
> "derivative," or else I present myself with that bold command:

"Make fresher?" Freshness is the most demanding task one faces when dealing with a traditional meter, no matter how forgiving that meter is.

The first several pages are a mess, but I like to allow the mess to flow and flower. I make it move, sitting back in my chair, rotating my shoulders every half hour or so; I try to unknot my muscles, go, go, go—as long as it is forward. Forget you are a sixty-seven-year-old woman with a girlish white pageboy. Forget all that business about fourteen lines of rhymed iambic pentameter; think of Leonardo and his sage wisdom: "Art breathes from containment and suffocates from freedom." Or the problems that accrue from the "weight of too much liberty" (Wordsworth). Drown out the noise of rhyme and rhythm. Think only of the small dramatic argument that's being brought into being—a handball court, or a courtroom itself, hard, demanding thick stone walls—between perseverance and its asymmetrical smash of opposition. Think of that rectangle, perfect in its proportions, that plastic cutlery tray in your kitchen drawer, with its sharp divisions for forks, knives, spoons. Or think of the shape of a human life, which, like it or not, is limited.

—*"Segue"*

Or perhaps you have seen a reprint of one of Susanna Moodie's letters. Here is an elusive life, but we can *know* her, italics again, and something of her times through her texts. Her sociological context comes drifting inevitably like snow, across the surface of what she writes. It is possible, for instance, to read a feminist consciousness through a text that denies any such thing. One of the other things we know is that letters in the middle of the nineteenth century were expensive to send and that they were paid for by the foolscap page. And so Susanna Moodie did what many of our thrifty early settlers did when writing a letter home to the old country: she indulged in cross-writing, writing her lines first horizontally on the page, then turning the paper and writing a second series of lines vertically. But Mrs. Moodie was also Mrs. Frugality, or Mrs. Resourceful, if you like, and turning her page forty-five degrees, she was able to write in a third cross, a diagonal set of lines. Her cheerful and generally newsy letters speak—forcefully—of all she did *not* set down: of poverty, desperation and an anxiety about connection at any inconvenience to herself and others. No wonder we read not just her books but these extraordinarily revealing letters. Furthermore, she lets slip now and then an unguarded, unedited thought that would never find room in a published book, and each of these "slips" becomes a cultural or personal moment that is secured, and that gestures toward a thousand other such moments. An author's papers, then—the letters, the drafts, the diaries, self-notations, and shopping lists, the photographs and drawings and audiotapes and publishers' catalogues—are collected for a reason. So that we can know about the *making* of the book and know also that the making and the being of a text are part of the same knit.

It is thought by some that the reader longs to be part of that knit out of a belief that the writer is holding hands with some god of creativity, or has a toe immersed in the creative source. To touch the writer is to touch, indirectly, that primal well. This seems to me a romantic notion that most writers would find hard to live up to. On the other hand, the reader's desire to "know" the writer and the writer's yoking of world and word, speaking from my own response as a reader, is one of vital, natural curiosity: how does the process move? What are the igniting forces? How is one idea linked to another? How is the writing illuminated by what is known of the writer's personal narrative—a narrative that can be at least partly pursued through a collection of working papers that are more or less (always qualifying here) available to anyone. So much in a writer's life is unwilled, capricious, inexplicable and unrecorded, but the small papery documents that accumulate on writers' desks are often capable of pointing to steps in the imaginative process. Behind the prose of a novel or the lines in a book of poems the author's personal narrative points toward the writer's unspoken reserves of thought or the sad or happy sea of a diurnal existence. The swirl of paper that surrounds a final draft is not just an extra suitcase taken on board to use up the weight allowance, but a demonstration of the distance a writer has travelled. Fiction possesses a puzzling inability to stare at itself—how did it get here, for instance, and what is its relation with reality—questions that these fragile, peripheral souvenirs of a writing life can assist us with.

Some writers are savers, some aren't, but most, when cautioned by archivists, become scrupulous with their scraps. I have to say that, from a writer's point of view, there is something disturbingly egocentric about this cherishing of one's personal minutiae and then the selling of these bits and pieces. At the same time, we are encouraged to believe we are a part of a useful enterprise that, aside from forming a picture of our society's culture, contributes to the charting of individual creative endeavours—although the archival record may greatly modify and streamline what is, in fact, a messy process relying on such non-recordable stimuli as weather, mood, accident or unexplained brain waves. No one fully understands the creative process, least of all writers. Virginia Woolf talks about her creative energy as that which "bubbles so pleasantly in beginning a new book" and that only later is transformed into "a tiresome bewildering distraction," as she wrote in her diary on Thursday, January 19, 1933.

Even so, we will never be able to reach through acid-free archival material to the *essence* of a writer. We all recognize that when a writer picks up a pen, a second self comes out, and this applies not just to manuscripts but to letters and even personal diaries. That which *seems unguarded* is in fact, in varying degree, composed, enhanced, deprecated, erased, or dressed for dinner. Freud once observed in a letter to Arnold Zweig: "Anyone turning biographer commits himself to lies, to concealment, to hypocrisy, to flattery, and even to hiding his own lack of understanding." He might very well have said the same thing about the raw materials of biography. There is reality on one side—though "reality," Nabokov tells us, is the only word in the language that always needs a set of quotation marks around it. And there is the author's *willed impression* of the world and the self the writer gives us: a smoke screen, a concealing cape, an occluded mirror, a kaleidoscope, a magic lantern, a lens polished with the self's self-conscious hand—the subjunctive self, which is perhaps all any of us can offer each other.

There is also the problem of the publicity machine, which turns writers into public creatures who do not resemble in any way the writing creature. Who, after all, is more skilful than the novelist when it comes to creating that nubby presence we refer to as *persona*. I never look at my book photos and bios without thinking: "What an interesting life that woman has. But who is she?"

I know who she is: she's my shadow self, my subjunctive self, a distant cousin who is only on nodding acquaintance with the person in the room with the shut door.

In Brief . . .

- More than one person sits down to write. Inside every writer is the performer, the creator, the storyteller. And seated next to her, or perhaps crouched inside her, is the source.

- The great world and the droplets that fall from it is the source of at least half a fiction writer's material.

- The use of public transportation can be extremely profitable to fiction writers, who are always looking to restock their supplies. And so are such public places as elevators or restaurants.

- We can't interrogate strangers, so we are forced to deal imaginatively with the great gaps. For novelists this means observing, listening at the keyhole as well as peering into it, gently probing, but in the end risking ourselves and our small truths, guessing at the way other people live and think, hoping to get it right at least part of the time.

- Where you write is less important than you think. Writers often perform their tasks in small rooms with the door closed. Their scenery is the interior life with its collection of images, discoveries, scenes, observations, dreams— that whole unwieldy cotton sack of material we refer to as memory.

- Save your papers; they document the creative process and show not just the top refined border of a writer's life and times, but the full depth of it. They show the making of the book.

~ 7 ~

PACING, PASSION AND TENSION

THE ADVICE WE REALLY NEED IS HOW BEST TO AVOID THE prescriptions, the wisdom, the rituals of other writers. And, yet, here I am, about to dump on you some of my ideas about the pacing and tension of fiction. The two go hand in hand. And I hope you'll remember that for every statement I may make, there are a hundred alternate ways in which you can pace a story, and that the further most writers go in their writing lives, the more liberties they feel able to take.

An example might be that old classic, the crime novel. Thirty years ago, it was possible to diagram a novel of this genre. You had a problem and a solution, and, between those two poles, a number of revelations, red herrings, and educations. The size of these internal structures escalated; the climax arriving at approximately page 135, followed by the wrap-up. But the crime novel has grown unruly. Sometimes the villain is named on the first page. Sometimes the body is discovered on the final page, and sometimes there is no body at all! The hardboiled cop is sometimes a soft-voiced professor, sometimes even reflective, sometimes even a woman, and sometimes gay.

Fiction, generally, is changing. The old problem/solution structure is harder to pin down, and a postmodern view holds that plot is the *enemy* of fiction, that characters, setting, theme, etc., get in the way of writing. It is harder and harder to say what a story is, but I *am* going to make an attempt at least. I think a story is about *moving from one state to another*, a movement that, in more interesting fiction, is psychological, involving a growth of awareness, a gathering of insight about what it means to be human.

Of course, this gathering of insight does not come in one flash, but in a series of revelations, revelations that come riding atop an important question. That question may, in some fiction, be only who murdered the ship's purser, or it may be, what is this story about?

By aboutness, I don't mean such facile descriptions as, for example: "this story is about a railway engineer who goes to London and meets a ballet dancer," or "this story is about an Alberta farm wife who decides to leave her husband in the middle of the haying season." These stories, to use the same two examples, are about 1. dislocation, 2. freedom and capability. Stories can often be reduced in this way to one or two words—what our old English teachers used to call themes—and the opening up of these ideas—the *how*, *why*, and *where* of it—is the question that hovers over the story from beginning to end, keeping the reader bonded to the text.

I have to say that not once during the writing of my own novels did it occur to me that I must worry about pacing or take responsibility for the creating and sustaining of tension. I can only suppose that I must have reasoned—with enormous arrogance—that, of course a reader would be glued to these pages of mine, since I, in the act of writing, was glued to the task at hand. I approached the typewriter each day with a combination of zeal and panic, and assumed, though I didn't articulate it, that something of that tension would spill onto the page. And this led to a fairly elementary conclusion—that the simple bonding of one's self to one's writing can create a sort of tension that no artificial plot ever will. A sense of urgency underlies certain books, a feeling that this story is being told because it *has* to be told.

A second insight came to me more painfully—and that was the discovery that a writer cannot speak to all audiences, cannot, that is, meet every reader's requirement in terms of tension. I don't *care*, for example, how the body got in the library. A terrible and cynical question—so what?—swims into my consciousness. Someone else may not care, though I do, about the famous, unhappy housewife Madame Bovary and whether or not she gets a measure of the sublime passion she craves. Jane Austen uses tension in one way and Helen MacInnes in another, but they are both doing one thing, which is *moving from one state to another*. Tension does not rely on an explicit sex scene every twenty-six pages, or on the reinforcement of so-called major themes. What it does rely on, to a very great extent, is that thing called pacing.

Pacing involves the *selection* and *placement* and *timing* of the variables of the story, the way in which the story is unrolled for the reader, the manner in which we move from revelation to revelation.

A number of problems arise in the pacing of a story. One of the most troublesome is the need a writer often feels to "frame" the story It's easy to see, especially in these postmodern days, why we have grown to distrust the narrative voice and therefore feel the need to justify it. So, instead of simply telling the story, a scaffolding is set up, a way into and out of the story. The relationship between the teller and the tale is laboriously worked up and is almost always in clumps and interfering. For example: a story about a woman who goes to a high school reunion and is reminded about an episode in her early life. She recounts the incident in the story. The last scene finds her back at the reunion, reflecting on the episode. The actual story has been buried, or shall we say, muffled. Another example: a Canadian soldier in Italy meets an Italian farmer and the farmer tells him a story about a ghost in the village. It's a good story, but by the time it's filtered through the Canadian soldier and the Italian farmer, there is very little immediacy left. Other examples: Stories found in discovered diaries. Stories overheard in restaurants. And stories that leak around the edges of memoirs. Normally, it's easy to edit these stories—a simple cutting of the first and last paragraph, the entrance and exit lopped off.

How does a writer confess that the printed offering is a tissue of imagination? The whole force of moral imperative rages against such a whimsical presentation: lying, inventing, daydreaming. In desperation early fiction writers supplied their narratives with implicitly understood framing devices like: This is a tale found in an old trunk. This is a story related to me by an ancient gentleman. This is a dream recorded by an angel.

We love fiction because it possesses the texture of the real. The characters in a novel resemble, more or less, ourselves. Fiction's dilemmas are similar to those we encounter every day, and there are novelists who do indeed write close to the autobiographical bone. As for the others, if they don't draw on their own experience, where on earth does it all come from?

There is a problem all fiction writers must face if they want to create unique and substantial characters. Characters, at least those personages who are going to be important to the developing narrative, require context. They can't simply be flung onto the page as though they had metamorphosed from warm mud. Darwin put an end to that. Freud too. Parthenogenesis doesn't work for human beings, not yet and probably never, unless being human becomes something other than what we know. Characters in books need to be supplied with a childhood of some sort, with parents at the very least, sometimes even grandparents.... Parents influence children, stiffening or weakening their resolve, and no credible novelist is going to reduce that assumption. Even in the most Kafkaesque dreamscape there are certain elements that cannot be subtracted from substance, geography, family, blood. Everyone is someone's child, and a novel, in the crudest of terms, is a story about the destiny of a child. There is always a bank of DNA pressing its claim....

In my view, it's not necessary to provide a complete genealogical chart; hardly any contemporary readers have the patience for that heft of information. Only a few vital family traces are required, the sense that the character isn't self-invented or arbitrary. Jane Austen, even though she is pre-Darwinian, always goes back at least one generation, and sometimes two. She knew the importance of grounding.

—Unless

This need to set the story in a context goes back to the Middle Ages and the beginning of fiction as we know it. Fiction was frowned upon by the Church, and thus stories often began with an apology, a lie, for example: "I found recorded in a very old book..." or "A traveller returned from several years at sea with this account..."

There may be times when we want to approach a story in this convoluted way, when we want to slow down or speed up the story. Certain themes require slower revelation. There is probably a reason why most police fiction is told swiftly and briefly—about a hundred and forty pages is average, I'm told. And why fantasy often requires four hundred pages. Knowing when to cut and when to thicken is important.

I'll talk about cutting first since it is something most of us find hard to do. There is still, floating around, a residue from the Hemingway ethos, the belief that a story must not contain one single extraneous detail, even though we all know that extraneous details give shading to character, furnish a scene, contribute to a sense of place and modify the tone of a piece. The right detail in the right place, though it impinges not at all on the movement of the story, can linger long after the story is forgotten. But overindulgence slows the story down and needs cutting, which is painful. A nice psychological trick is not to cross out, but to *cut* out with scissors, store your verbiage in your files and kid yourself that this is something you might want to use someday.

Cutting does tidy a story, increases the pace, and it can—and this is something to bear in mind—change its nature. I was once asked to cut a 110-minute play to a 40-minute one-act piece. The play, once a social comedy, is now a breakneck farce. There is almost no shading, but I have to confess, it has a kind of hectic energy that may be just as valuable.

Thickening is something else, and it leads me to what I see as one of the most persistent problems in fiction—the failure to understand that fiction is made up of scenes. Very often scenes are merely sketched; there are too many of them and they are almost invariably rushed. Unlike the scenes we're accustomed to in film, the scenes in fiction have to be more than a fleeting image. They have to be solidly built and furnished. They have to be introduced, allowed to develop and conclude in such a way that the next scene is prepared for.

Part of scene-making comes from details of place, and I think this is what Jane Austen does so superbly. We all know what is going to happen in a Jane Austen novel: a young woman of marriageable age pursues and captures that singular object, the marriageable male. Why do we keep turning those pages? I think it is because Austen is able to build a world, albeit small, that we can enter and where we can be certain of our footing. The solidity of that world is amazing. It has a top, a bottom, and a precisely outlined perimeter. There are rules—and every breach of the rules is pointed out. There is a small cast of characters, and any intrusion from the outside is identified as an intrusion. The small excitements of each scene become ours; all the proportions are right. We, many of us anyway, can be thankful that Jane Austen didn't set her novels in Tahiti or Hong Kong or we might have lost the treasure of her village-world and our participation in the scenes she provides.

Where then did Jane Austen find the material for her novel? Every writer draws on his or her own experience; where else could the surface details of a novel's structure come from, especially a novel as assured in its texture as *Pride and Prejudice*? But it is not every novelist's tactic to draw *directly* on personal narrative, and Jane Austen, clearly, is not a writer who touches close to the autobiographical core.

—*Jane Austen: A Life*

Besides a sense of place and a secure placing in time, a scene can be expanded, thickened, and sustained by the use of dialogue, that most immediate of story variables, dialogue that reveals character, moves the story forward, and provides, sideways as it were, the pieces of information we need, which would otherwise sound self-conscious in the narrator's mouth.

How long, it might be asked, should a scene be sustained? As long as it is still level, inventive, beguiling and yielding answers to that important overriding question I mentioned earlier: what is this story about? The development of scenes, besides prodding writers into the concrete, non-abstract world, and besides opening up dramatic possibilities, also makes the lot of the writer easier. The story falls into manageable units once the concept of scenes is grasped, and one is less likely to feel overwhelmed by a huge mass of material. A scene at a time. A step at a time.

> There is what the literary tribe calls a "set piece," a jewel, as it were, set in a spun-out text, or a chunk of narrative that is somehow more intense, more cohesive, more self-contained than the rest. Generally theatrical and vivid, it can be read and comprehended, even when severed from the wider story, or it can be "performed"...
> —*"Flitting Behavior"*

Occasionally, the pace is distorted by what I think of as a failure of transformation. All writers draw on their own experiences, though very few, I think, draw directly. The reason it is *fiction* and not *autobiography* is because an act of transformation has taken place. Sometimes this involves relocation or renaming or reshaping or, most importantly, reinterpretation and re-imagining. Occasionally, the process is incomplete. You know you're dealing with this problem if there is an element in the story that seems to belong in another story. But, the writer says in defence, this is how it really happened. I remember once seeing a story in which there was a rather awkward page in which a woman character heard a doorbell ring and had to go down a flight of steep stairs to answer the door. The story slowed down at this point. Why not have the woman on the ground floor? I asked the writer. *Because that's the way it happened*, the writer said, and seemed unable to see outside the pattern already incised on the experience and then on the story.

Moving people around in space, as a matter of fact, can be tedious and often adds fat to the narrative. There is a wonderful V. S. Pritchett story in which a character receives a letter from a woman who has a piece of information for him. Will he come to the city where she lives? The next paragraph starts along the lines, "Two hours later he was on her doorstep..." I marvelled at this neat solution. I would have had him putting on his overcoat, backing the car out of the garage, getting onto the highway, consulting a street map, and so on, and for what reason?

An important part of pacing is releasing pertinent information at exactly the right moment, and not too much at one time in case the reader feels force-fed. Sometimes Alice Munro's stories stop in the middle and the narrator says, "I forgot to tell you that..." Now, she hasn't forgotten to tell you at all. It is only *now* that she wants you to have the information. This is not the same thing as teasing the reader, but it clashes with Dickens' old bit of advice: "Keep them laughing, keep them waiting."

The handling of time, in fiction, is extraordinarily difficult, and I speak as someone who is still struggling with this. One summer, not long ago, dismayed by my bank balance, I read a number of popular bestsellers, the kind of fiction that is called drugstore fiction, the kind you buy by the pound to carry off to the beach. The common element I found in these books was the unimaginative handling of time. Chronology was strictly adhered to, a conveyor belt straight into the future, this despite the fact that we know the human mind is frequently dwelling on the past and on the future and only occasionally on the present. Interesting and complex time structures occur in almost all serious fiction, but they are difficult to make credible or acceptable.

It's important to trust the reader, but many readers are less than a hundred percent conscientious and forgiving and so they must be placed firmly in time. I think it's a good idea for beginning writers to set their works in manageable time chunks. Chapters that begin "Sixty years later..." tend to ask a great deal.

The mismanagement of flashbacks is another problem, and transition seems to be the key. Past action must be carefully introduced and not allowed to swallow up a disproportionate part of the story. For example, it would be unwieldy if a story of three thousand words were to have a thousand words cast in the past. There must also be, I think, a *reason* for a time diversion. Perhaps some piece of information must be supplied. Is there another way it can be done? Perhaps in a section of dialogue dealing with the past. Perhaps a brief paragraph of meditation on a past event would be less disruptive than moving the actual narrative to the past. If flashbacks are what you decide on, I think a piece of fiction is better balanced if there is a pattern of some kind. If there is a single flashback in an entire novel, there is a danger of unbalancing the whole ship. If there are several flashbacks, fairly evenly spaced and of somewhat the same length, the reader will come to anticipate and accept them more readily and be less likely to be thrown into a state of confusion.

Another problem: that little bundle of words that gets us to those other places and times is ridden with clichés. The word "meanwhile" makes us think "meanwhile, back at the ranch . . ." "Suddenly" seems hokey. Also: "at that moment" or "the next thing he knew" or "without further ado" or "his thoughts drifted back to . . ."

All writers know about the magic of opening sentences, the golden door that takes you into the story, pushes at the future and nudges your expectations, setting the tone and carrying you over that threshold into the fictional world. These sentences work best when they carry on their back an implied question. One of my favourites is John Cheever's "Each year, we rent a house at the edge of the sea." That *we*. A married person's we? *Each year*—the cycle of habit suggested. *Rented*, not owned—more information. A *house*, not a cottage—a suggestion of class, of wealth. The *sea*, not the ocean or the lake—an unnamed sea—a suggestion of East Coast perhaps. And the implied question—how will the statement be subverted? What will happen this year to alter the smooth presumption of the announcement—*Each year, we rent a house at the edge of the sea.*

It's easy to get too cute, too obvious, about an arresting first sentence, and it is wise to avoid such openings as: "'Jesus,' Mavis said, opening the envelope, 'not again!'" or "Ronald knew the minute he woke up that it was going to be one of those days" or "It was midnight when we arrived in the empty flat, and the first thing we saw was a note pinned to the door."

Pacing can be controlled to some extent by the skilled use of breaks. This means knowing where to break and start a new chapter, and also where to break a paragraph. These breaks, I think, act as miniature signposts, allowing the reader, subconsciously perhaps, to feel out the pattern and order in a work, and this feeling of order gives assurances that one is not wandering in an unmapped jungle. Mavis Gallant, who frequently writes rather long paragraphs, will occasionally throw in a paragraph composed of one short line, or even one word—a signal that something important is happening. She is underlining something for you, telling you to pay attention.

There is an old saying that the climax of a piece of fiction should come shortly before the end. You probably *do* need one major event or confrontation. This need not be a scene in which there is a physical upheaval, but merely, perhaps, an unfolding of understanding. Generally, some planning must go into the generating of this scene—a number of smaller scenes may build toward it. There should be some foreshadowing, those little brushstrokes of possibility, so that when the dénouement does arrive, it will both surprise and satisfy some level of expectation.

There are many kinds of endings, those that reach back into the story and restate what has happened, or those that go sliding off the page, taking a chance, risking the subversion of the story, but suggesting some new pattern in which the events of the story may be imagined.

There are stories we read quickly, others we read slowly, and again and again. Style, a quirky syntax, a challenging vocabulary help set the speed, but ultimately it is the writer's ability to communicate with passion that keeps the eyes moving along the lines of print and the pages turning over.

In Brief . . .

The crucial elements:

- **Story:** A story is about moving from one state to another, a movement that may be psychological, involving a growth of awareness that comes in a series of revelations.
- **Tension:** The simple bonding of one's self to one's writing can create tension, that sense of urgency that underlies certain books, a feeling that this story is being told because it has to be told.
- **Pacing:** Pacing involves the selection and placement and timing of the variables of the story, the way in which the story is unrolled for the reader, the manner in which it moves from revelation to revelation. An important part of pacing is releasing pertinent information at exactly the right moment; too much at one time can make the reader feel force-fed. Pacing can be controlled to some extent by the skilled use of breaks.
- **Framing:** Framing is often unnecessary; it can bury or muffle a story. It can be easy to edit out the framing—a simple cutting of the first and last paragraphs.
- **Cutting:** The right detail in the right place can linger long after the story is forgotten. But cutting extraneous detail can tidy a story and increase its pace, and can also change its nature.
- **Dialogue:** Dialogue provides a sense of place and time. It reveals character, moves the story forward, and provides

information we need that would sound self-conscious in the narrator's mouth.

- **Scenes:** One of the most persistent problems in fiction is the failure to understand that a story is made up of scenes. Scenes have to be more than a fleeting image. They have to be solidly built and furnished. They have to be introduced, allowed to develop and conclude in such a way that the next scene is prepared for. Sustain a scene for as long as it is still level, inventive, beguiling and yielding answers to what this story is about. Scenes help the story fall into manageable units. A scene at a time; a step at a time.

- **Transformation:** A story is fiction and not autobiography because an act of transformation has taken place. Sometimes this involves relocation, renaming or reshaping or, most importantly, reinterpretation and re-imagining.

- **Time:** It is difficult to handle time in fiction. Interesting and complex time structures occur in almost all serious fiction, but a good idea for beginning writers is to set your works in manageable time chunks. Past action must be carefully introduced and not allowed to swallow up a disproportionate part of the story.

- **Opening sentences:** Opening sentences take you into the story, push at the future and nudge your expectations, setting the tone and carrying you over that threshold into the fictional world. These sentences work best when they carry an implied question.

- **Climax:** You probably do need one major event or confrontation—this need not be a physical upheaval; it can be an unfolding of understanding. Some planning must go into generating this scene—a number of smaller scenes may build toward it, some foreshadowing, little brushstrokes of possibility, so that when the dénouement does arrive, it will both surprise and satisfy some level of expectation.

- **Endings:** Endings may reach back into the story and restate what has happened, or go sliding off the page, taking a chance, risking the subversion of the story, but suggesting some new pattern in which the events of the story may be imagined.

- **Style:** A quirky syntax, a challenging vocabulary, help set the speed, but ultimately it is the writer's ability to communicate with passion that keeps the eyes moving along the lines of print and the pages turning over.

~ *8* ~

WHERE CURIOSITY LEADS

THERE WAS A PERIOD IN MY EARLY LIFE WHEN MY FRIENDS AND
I, spurred by romantic yearnings, I suppose, spent great widths of
time talking about the possibility and need of "truly knowing someone." The phrase chimed with half a dozen others in our vocabulary:
the exposing of the soul, the opening of the heart, the completion of
one person by another, and so forth. We believed this kind of intimate knowledge was possible, and moreover that it was desirable.

Somewhere along the way, I lost faith with the enterprise. What
interested me, instead, was the *unknowability* of others, their very
otherness, in fact. It was apparent to me that members of close, loving families resisted the forces of coercive revelation, and that even
partners in long, happy marriages remained, ultimately, strangers,
one to the other. Although we are living in the age of communica-
tion, it became clear that people who "spilled their guts" sacrificed
a portion of their dignity in so doing, and that, in any case, what
they spilled was suspect, either self-pitying or self-aggrandizing, or
else projecting a single, touched-up version of who they were and
how they preferred to be registered at a particular moment—for

it was understood that a variant self could be brought forward the next day, or even the next hour.

It might be thought that I would be dismayed to discover the limited nature of human interaction, but instead I was heartened, in the same way I was heartened, and relieved too, when I realized that the Methodist God, with whom I'd grown up, did not necessarily observe every ripple of sensation that passed through my head. To be *known* was to be incapacitated, and stripped bare. To be solitary, that is, to be left in a state of privacy, was to hang on to the forces of originality and innocence.

We are born alone, we die alone: those two austere existential declaratives were a comfort to me as I grew to adulthood. But to be alone in the midst of life brought to the table a degree of solitude that required a certain amount of philosophical accommodation. I found the premise, in fact, close to unbearable. Human activity with its random jets of possibility and immobilization was the oxygen I sought. The hum of human busyness engaged me at every level; it was what illuminated my imagination and what found its way into my novels. My own life—what a sorry admission, and yet it was true!—was not quite enough. I desperately needed to know how other people lived, how they moved about from room to room in their ordinary houses and gardens, what ordinary or extraordinary things they said to each other and to themselves as the clock struck midnight or 9 a.m. or noon, even though I saw my curiosity about such things as lying side-by-side with the idleness of gossip or the wasteful longing of voyeurism.

Judith Gill, the narrator of *Small Ceremonies*, announces her need openly, that she requires for her survival the narratives of other lives, and that she is willing to suspend judgment and direction and moral imperative in order to do nothing more than peer into the windows of alternate human arrangements. Her need is so strong, in fact, that she becomes a professional biographer, a vocation that allows her to snoop, sniff, interview, eavesdrop, interpret and bring to ripe conclusion the motives and figurative possibilities of her subjects.

When I first began writing novels, friends asked me what it was I wrote about. At first I didn't know what to say, for, in fact, I wasn't sure what my subject was. I soon found out—by reading reviews of my books, and listening to these same friends.

It seemed I wrote about ordinary people—whoever *they* are—and their ordinary, yet occluded, lives. And I also wrote, more and more, about that subjunctive branch of people (*mea culpa*) who were curious about the details of *other* ordinary people, so curious, in fact, that they became biographers or novelists, those beings who are allowed societal permission to investigate—through the troughs of archival material, through letters and diaries and blurred photographs, by way of offhand conversations and reminiscences and abrupt literary interpolations and fictional thrusts directed at the lives of the famous and the not-at-all famous.

How do we arrive, then, at the lives of others, their assumed kernel of authenticity? As a child, I did poorly at mathematics, but enjoyed what we called "story problems." Mary Brown is sent to the grocer's for two pounds of cheese at a dollar and a half a pound. How much change will she get back from a $20 bill? The answer came easily, or not so easily, but it was the tug of biographical curiosity I chiefly felt. Who was this Mary Brown and what was she doing with all that cheese? Was she old enough to be trusted with a $20 bill? And what of her wider dreams and aspirations, or even her immediate thoughts as she skipped home with her sack of groceries and her pocketful of coins?

I remember trying to "interview" my Canadian mother-in-law when she was in her eighties, wanting to access a portion of the childhood she had spent on a pioneer farm in Manitoba. The project was doomed from the beginning. I didn't know the right questions, and she didn't have any idea what I wanted to know. My line of inquiry, even to my own ears, felt intrusive and inappropriate, and her answers were, not surprisingly, vague and, for my purposes, not at all useful. What I hoped for was the precise, inch-by-inch texture of that early twentieth century Icelandic farmhouse located on a threadlike river sixty miles north of Winnipeg, the furniture, the floor coverings, the ceiling, the ornaments that rested on the rough kitchen shelves. What I got were generalities: *Well, it was homey. Well, we made our own cheese. The sheep, they were a bother. It was cold in winter.* In short, the experiment was a failure. I half expected it would be.

There is something oddly shaming about possessing so avid a sense of curiosity.

Naturally when I find myself on buses or trains, I feel a compulsion to know the titles of the books my fellow passengers are reading. And when I am being interviewed about one of my books, I often find myself interviewing back: *How did you happen to become a journalist? What sort of articles are you usually assigned? Do you have any children? Tell me more.*

More is what the indecently curious always want. They want the *details*, and no detail is too small to be of interest.

Speaking of curiosity, I was talking to some women friends, and we got onto the subject of wondering what it's like to be a man at the end of our century.

I started asking some of the men I knew this question and I started writing a novel called *Larry's Party*.

My informal survey wasn't always successful. Almost every man I put this question to rebounded by saying, "Well, but—I'm not a typical man." And therein may lie the path to understanding. Other men went immediately into their jocularity mode—and I knew what that meant, that they were strenuously avoiding any kind of serious thinking on the subject.

But some men listened thoughtfully and replied candidly; a few confessed to me that they had never had this discussion before and that they welcomed it, and they hoped I'd be patient if their response came awkwardly framed. Their lives had not always been predictable, not easy or settled, not as anchored as their fathers' lives, and certainly not accompanied by the same guarantees of authority.

I've always been interested in men and women and the curious ways they are matched and mismatched in the world. Toni Morrison talks in one of her essays about the split consciousness of most Americans, and the fact that this splitting is caused by an ever-present consciousness of race, the guilty and haunting sense of "the other."

But my "other" was men. What they were, who they were or what they wanted, despite having a father, a brother, a husband, a son, and a few—not a lot but a few—men friends. And as I wrote *Larry's Party* I thought often of the immense mysteries men keep from women. And the mysteries women keep from men.

I do think it's important that men try to write about women and women about men. Otherwise we'll end up with two separate literatures, just as, I'm told, we have girl movies these days and boy movies. Perhaps our literature is already segregated. You can test this thesis by asking your friends who Jo March is. Almost no men know the answer to that question; almost all women do.

Yet we all know that a fully furnished universe is made up of men and women, and that women writers are often called upon to write about men, and male writers about women. Writers go even further at times, not just writing about the other sex, but speaking through its consciousness as I tried to do in *Larry's Party*.

The question can be asked, and often is, how successful is this gender-hopping? Does any truth at all seep through? Maybe more than we think. Oscar Wilde had the notion that we can hear more of the author's true voice in her or his fictional impersonations than we can in any autobiography, not that he bothered with the niceties of gender pronouns. "Man is least himself," he said, "when he talks in his own person. Give him a mask, and he will tell you the truth." A mask, he said, but he might also have said a skirt. Or, for women writers, a small pointy beard.

"You're not really going to write about a man called Larry, are you?" my daughter said.* The name Larry reminded her of someone standing in a sixties rec room wearing polyester pants.

I was pleased with this description; it was exactly what I wanted.

Who is this Larry Weller from Winnipeg and what's he like? He's growing up, for one thing, emerging from today's long, long childhood. He's born in the year 1950 and the novel takes him from age

---

* Anne is certain she was the daughter; she remembers the conversation. It is possible, though, that one of her other sisters made the same observation and that this may have led to a similar discussion.

twenty-six right up to the present. He has two parents, two wives, one son, a sister, a handful of friends.

He's someone trying to be a good man in a world that doesn't always encourage him to think in terms of goodness. And I wanted to give him some dignity, having observed that men in movies and on TV have become buffoons: when did this happen? My first draft didn't quite manage this dignity, and I had to go through the final draft with a small piece of sandpaper, as it were, restoring him to himself and to my initial image of who he is.

I knew I'd have to have some male furniture, cars and sports in the book, areas I usually avoid, out of ignorance and also disinclination. But what concerned me far more was trying to understand how the thought synapses in a man's head work. We talk about the linear male mode and the circular female style, but I knew that was too simple. Of course I worried about getting it right, but I comforted myself by remembering that I was only writing about one man, not *men.*

And then there's that question of body. The sexes can learn a lot about each other by patient observation and by sympathy, but in the end that other body is the place men and women can't quite go. Nevertheless, since this is a novel about a man, there is a chapter called "Larry's Penis."

There are other chapters called "Larry's Folks," "Larry's Work," "Larry's Love," "Larry's Friends"—fifteen of these chapters that move forward in time and also, I like to think, provide a kind of CAT scan look at Larry Weller's life. An ordinary life, if there is such a thing.

I fell into discussion with two male writers while I was working on the book, Jack Hodgins and John Ralston Saul, and they asked me if I had written about Larry's clothes. Well, no, I said, I hadn't thought his clothes were important. They convinced me, though, and I'm grateful, that socks and underwear and tie choices are part of the male profile, and so there is a chapter called "Larry's Threads."

While I was thinking of the problems of men and women, I was also pursuing my interest in mazes and labyrinths. It happened that a few years ago I was walking across a public park in Saffron Walden in England and found myself standing in the middle of a medieval turf maze, one of the most famous in the world, though I'd never heard of it.

I started, then, reading about mazes, and visiting those I was able to. There are all sorts of theories about why mazes, these doodles on the earth's skin, exist. They're found in almost every culture and corner of the world, hedge mazes, stone mazes, engravings on rocks or on ancient coins. They may be symbols of the turnings and twistings of life. A way to represent the birth journey or the journey to God. Some are probably sexual in meaning, a part of courtship rituals, or else they're games, diversions, distractions from the hardships of existence.

It seemed natural to give Larry Weller my passion for mazes. He becomes, gradually, a designer of mazes—and so this ordinary man has an extraordinary profession. In fact, there are only about a dozen maze makers in the world, but their impact is being felt as more and more contemporary mazes are being constructed.

Writing this novel I thought of each chapter as a small maze with an entrance and an exit, and it is in the final chapter, called "Larry's Party," where Larry confronts the major maze of his life, the maze of love and of being loved, of permanence, of wisdom, and, in a sense, of a return to the knowledge of his self.

The editing of this novel was a peculiar pleasure. The line editor lived in a cottage in the wolds of Oxfordshire, and, since we'd both discovered email at the same time, we decided to go about our day-to-day negotiations using this amazing technology, so much more immediate than a fax and more satisfying than the telephone.

Of course with three English-language publishers working together, there were wrinkles to work out. My chapter called "Larry's Shingle," in which Larry goes into business for himself, was completely unintelligible to the UK publisher, who thought shingles were those stones that lie about on the beaches. We settled for "Larry Inc." as the chapter title.

And there were questions of historical accuracy. Three editors thought I was fantasizing when I had Larry drinking cappuccino in Winnipeg back in 1977. I phoned a friend of mine, Mark Morton, who had just published a book about food, and asked him. "Give me half an hour," he said, and came back with the information that an Italian café had brought cappuccino to Winnipeg in the fifties, though it was a café from which women were casually excluded.

One morning there was an urgent email from England about a scene in which Brussels sprouts are eaten, at an August Sunday dinner in Chapter 3. Brussels sprouts don't appear in the market until October, the editor said, so I would either have to change the month or the vegetable. "Nonsense," came the word from New York—an editor who buys her Brussels sprouts frozen in a little box any time of the year she chooses.

We did, in fact, move the scene to October, but I marvelled over the fact that a novel devolves in the last days of its shaping to questions of Brussels sprouts and their proper season.

In Brief . . .

Getting other people right:
- It's important that men try to write about women and women about men. Otherwise we'll end up with two separate literatures.
- If your first draft doesn't quite capture the character you mean to create, you might need to go through the final draft with a small piece of sandpaper, restoring your character to your initial image of who he or she is.

~ 9 ~

THE LOVE STORY

To be a romantic is to believe anything can happen to us.
THE REPUBLIC OF LOVE

LIKE MOST CHILDREN I STARTED OUT BELIEVING ROMANTIC
love belonged to the world of fairy stories and Saturday afternoon matinees, but I had the good luck, once, to witness my
uncle bending over at the dining room table to kiss the back of
my aunt's neck. It was summer time, and she was wearing a sun-
dress and just lifting a spoonful of sherbet to her lips. They were
middle-aged then, probably in their fifties, and I was a child of
nine or ten—but, with a delicious shudder, I recognized "it": love,
tenderness, ardour, romance, ravishment. All that was desirable
and baffling, and, in this tight domestic space of our dining room,
so utterly surprising.

Despite this revelation I very early fell into the trap of believing love and intelligence lived on different sides of the track. Silly
folks fell in love, and love itself was a manic, puppyish disease from

which people were expected to recover, assuming in time their roles as responsible citizens.

One night, not many years ago, I found my daughter rummaging in my bookshelves. She was exasperated. "Don't you have any love stories?" she asked.*

Love, after all, was what all of us wanted, yearned for, even at times died for, so why wasn't it showing its face on the publishing lists? It struck me that the problem was partly one of language; the syntax of love has been co-opted by pop culture—rock lyrics, greeting cards—just as the language of ardour had been taken over by the porn industry. To see the word *kiss* or *embrace* was to invite a flush of embarrassment.

More serious, perhaps, was the profound skepticism about the components of love—the sense that love was no more than a cocktail of chemicals and momentary encounters and sentimental echoes, leading inevitably back to the blackness of alienation and betrayal. To produce A Love Novel was to dabble, to sentimentalize, to enter the realm of triviality.

My own attempt to write A Love Novel, *The Republic of Love,* published in 1992, was summed up in the *Oxford Companion to Canadian Literature* as "a good humoured urban fantasy." This is either a monumental misreading—the book is as much about loneliness as it is about love—or an expression of profound cynicism: love as illusion, as wistful fantasy. Do we really believe this, that romantic love no longer powers and transforms ourselves and our society? Have we announced that the written word and perceived world are permanently disconnected? (The no-longer-quotable Woody Allen

---

* We have no idea which daughter this might have been.

has commented on how writers of comedy are always seated at the children's table; if this is true, writers who attempt The Love Story are seated *beneath* the table.)

Once The Love Story held parity with The Story of Good and Evil, and it manifested itself in subtle ways. Consider Jane Austen's use (non-use, really) of body parts in her books. (Fortunately there is a concordance available to help you out.) There are something like two ankles and one nose in all of her six novels. Also three breasts—though these breasts belong exclusively to men and represent the seat of fine feeling and not the heaving bosoms of female passion. And so the rise on Austen's romantic thermometer is signalled *obliquely*, a flutter of a hand standing in for a major amorous response, and all of it on a curious miniaturized scale, like looking into a doll's house of sensuality.

It may be that a permissive society allows us to say whatever we like now, and so there is no longer a prohibitive, punishing construct to push against. Or it may be that gender shifts in the last half-century have bred distrust. Or that loveless sex has spread widths of confusion and grief. Or that Erich Segal's version of The Love Story made us wary and unwilling to be taken in again. Or that fiction often feeds on inferior fiction, not life, with love scenes no larger than quick retakes of what we glimpse through the Hollywood keyhole, and pillow talk coming straight out of the beaten meringue of the Harlequin universe. Look out for the brilliant young soap-opera physician about to perform brain surgery on his ex-wife. He's been given all the bad lines, and they've led love straight into contempt.

It may be that The Love Story has lost credibility because we've gone back to the notion of the self who is endlessly in conversation with the self, imprisoned in the flesh of the self and denied by biology and logic the redemption of love, the comfort of the embrace of another. The Venerable Bede, the seventh century historian and theologian, once compared a human life to a swallow that flies by accident out of the darkness and into the lighted banquet hall, then swiftly crosses the brilliant beamed space, and darts out the other end, back into the night. This is a compelling and reasonable image; it sings beautifully to the tune of our own sad times. But how much richer in potential is the notion of that bird flying side by side with another, their wings almost but not quite touching, the two of them guided by an inexplicable binary radar, and an instinctive wish to join their lives together.

I wanted to see what was possible, and so I wrote A Love Story, *The Republic of Love*, set in Winnipeg.

In Brief . . .

- The Love Story may have lost credibility, but consider the notion of a bird flying through life side by side with another, their wings almost but not quite touching, the two of them guided by an inexplicable binary radar, and an instinctive wish to join their lives together. That is a story worth risking.

~ *10* ~

THE SHORT STORY (AND WOMEN WRITERS)

WHEN ROBERTO CALASSO'S BOOK *The Marriage of Cadmus and Harmony* came out it was interesting to watch editors squirm as they tried to figure out which list to put it on. Fiction or non-fiction, this mix of folklore, history, poetry, narrative, commentary. Which was it? All of the above? Or none of the above?

The confusion was affirming rather than disturbing for someone who's loved literature from childhood, but has never felt comfortable with its forms and definitions. Consider how we define prose: writing that is not poetry. And what is poetry? Writing that is not prose, of course. Consider that puzzling non-name-brand: non-fiction. A short story as everyone knows is a prose narrative that can be read in a single sitting, never mind what that quaint abstraction, a single sitting, means. A novel is the same thing except longer, like several sittings presumably. How long is a novel or a story? About as long as a piece of string. A narrative is, well, a story, and a story is—a narrative, of course.

There are other problems besides definitions. Every detail in a short story must contribute to its total effect; Chekhov and

Hemingway said so, so it had to be true. A story had to have conflict, that old word. It took some time to understand just what a
set-up the ascending storyline was, and how little of the texture
and boldness of life, of women's lives in particular, could be shaped
to fit its contours.

In my attitudes toward fiction, one shoe dropped, then another,
then a shower of shoes. A very large shoe fell the day I heard Helen
Buss, an academic from the University of Calgary—this would be
1983 or so—dismiss the binaries of tragedy and comedy as relics from
the patriarchy (and I promised myself I wouldn't use that word). At
a literary conference, I listened to a number of very serious aca-
demics discuss whether Susanna Moodie's *Roughing It in the Bush*
was a novel or a series of sketches or a memoir or what? Needless
to say, nothing was concluded at the end of this discussion, and it
seemed to me that those learned souls who were fretting about the
genre of Mrs. Moodie's work were missing the whole book, which
makes its own shape, makes it up as it goes along, inventing and
rearranging and pushing toward something new.

I began in the early eighties, while writing a series of short stories called *Various Miracles*, to swerve away from the easy comfort
zone of so-called epiphanies that accounted for the traditional
rondure of short stories, those abrupt but carefully prepared-for
lurches toward awareness, the manipulative wrap-up that arrived
like a hug in the final paragraph.

Resolution in itself began to feel false, the Grail, the Goal (with
capital Gs), large noble gestures, sudden blinding insight, an exaggeration and level of heat that is the equivalent of hurled crockery
or a burst of sunlight.

Instead I wanted stories that soared off into mystery and disruption, not mere flat openness but a spiralling into space or a melting into another narrative as happens at the end of a story I wrote titled "Home." Or I would fast-forward the final paragraph into the future, something that occurs in another story called "Flitting Behavior." Or dive with it into the past, which is the kind of ending that occurs in a piece called "Scenes." I wanted these endings to hold an aesthetic surprise that spun *off* the narrative, but wasn't necessarily generated *out* of it.

I tried in the short story "Scenes" to dislocate the spine of a traditional story, that holy line of rising action that is supposed to lead somewhere important, somewhere inevitable, modelled perhaps on the orgasmic pattern of tumescence followed by detumescence, an endless predictable circle of desire, fulfillment, and quiescence. I was for some reason drawn to randomness and disorder, not circularity or narrative cohesion. In fact, I had observed how the human longing for disruption was swamped in fiction by an almost mechanical model of aesthetic safety.

> I had an argument with Matt Cohen about how long a book of
> short stories should be. He thinks 150 pages is about right (and
> that's what he's doing) but I want more than 200 pages, a real book
> feel to it.
>
> —*Letter to Anne Giardini*

I had started in the early eighties to pay attention to the way in which women, sitting around a table for instance, tell each other stories. I noticed that they dealt in the episodic, and tended to suppress what was smoothly linear, to set up digressions, little side stories, often of a genealogical nature, which were not really digressions at all but integral parts of the story, to throw into the kitty. One time such a conversation was about the dolls we had played with as girls. Every anecdote we exchanged had a different structure and feel to it, but afterward I wondered if they didn't add up to a larger, more complex image, an image that commented in its prismatic way on the nature of women and their ability to care for something beyond themselves, and in their concern create a strategy for survival.

Out of that discussion came a story called "Dolls, Dolls, Dolls, Dolls," the title nodding, I hoped, to the collective nature of stories. John Barth makes the point in his 1994 novel *Once upon a Time: A Floating Opera* that the central narrative question for the fiction writer is not "what happens?" but "who am I?" Many women would modify that statement slightly, framing it as "who are we?"

In 1984 I wrote a story called "A Wood" in collaboration with my daughter, Anne Giardini. She was visiting; we wanted to spend as much time together as possible, but I had a deadline for a book of stories. I suggested we try to do one together. We agreed on a procedure. I would write one page and hand it over to Anne, who would write the next page, then hand it back to me. We were allowed to make two or three small changes to each other's pages. After seventeen days we agreed that we had a sort of story, and we sat down together to edit it. The story is not a seamless whole—that seemed beyond us—but is broken instead into seventeen related segments. It is an odd and slippery story and has something of the linguistic roughness you see in translations. I included it in the manuscript I submitted, thinking they would probably see it as an authorial anomaly and delete it from the book. But the issue of joint authorship never came up, and the story appeared along with the others, along with a note that it was written "With Anne Shields."*

We're always hearing (to deal with a major myth) that there are more women writers than men around, as though women were somehow engaged in an aggressive conspiracy to take over. It's interesting that no one ever goes around saying how odd it is that there are so many male writers around. This has been going on for a long time. In 1853, J. M. Ludlow advised his British readers, "But we *have* to notice [regard the coercion] the fact, that at this particular period of the world's history, the very *best* novels in several great countries happen to have been written by women." And a CBC producer apparently remarked to Margaret Atwood a few years ago, "A number of us are upset because we feel women are taking over the Canadian literary scene." Is this paranoia? And what is it based on? There are still plenty of men writing and being published but somewhere there is a tide turning, and it may just be here.

And if this is so, let me move quickly to the question of quality. Why does it seem—and again this is difficult to prove—that the Canadian short story is flourishing around the world and that women are contributing to that flowering? Some of it must be put down to a random dispensation of talent, which makes it presumptuous to speculate on the why and how of an Alice Munro or Mavis Gallant: we just have to be grateful to have them. On the other hand, we're all familiar with the history of the short story as we know it. It began with Poe and Hawthorne, and is a child of the New World. It's almost as though newly opened regions clamour,

---

* "I think it will give the book that special touch of weirdness I'm becoming so fond of," Carol wrote to Anne that year. "Why, I wonder."

not for old tales and myths, but for an account of present moments of experience. Maybe now the frontier has shifted, shifted northward and westward, but shifted most dramatically to that previously unfranchised half of the human race whose experiences were mostly buried in journals and letters, and in that perverted but courageous old creature, the potboiler.

There are a few myths about women's writing that can be put under the sod. That women excel at the short story because they write out of fragmented experience, between batches of biscuits or tubs of laundry. That women write short stories because they're forever signing up for creative writing courses down at the Y that concentrate on the short story form. That something diminutive about the size of women, and something unspoken and fluffy predisposes them to shorter forms and prohibits them from diving into more epic work. That the precision, dexterity, compression, and frugality of the female imagination serve the short story form, as does something else called the female voice in literature.

The female imagination is problematic because it brings to mind something monumental and eternal when in fact it is only what is concerning women at a particular time, a constantly changing and developing pool of ideas or images or whatever, which *some* women, *in general, from time to time, may* share.

And I would be happy to embrace the altogether attractive myth of the feminine voice. It is tempting to believe that delicacy, fluidity, subtlety, and elegance are more pronounced in the writing of women. We would be gladly served by the belief that women are masters of rich language patterns, intricate clustered metaphors or a syntax that is artful, supple, and suggestive—but can we prove it?

What we do often find in women's work is worth paying attention to. A time that we may describe as present and personal and urgent. Often too, the emotional range is wider. There is perhaps less exaggeration, less mythologizing. Settings tend to be simple but universal: enclosures, rooms, houses. Crossing borders, in any direction, we can find a commonality of subject matter, subject matter made accessible by the fact of its being rooted in the lives of women and easily translatable from one culture to another. It is a universal truth, for example, that the majority of women have been mothers and therefore witnesses to the growth and development of human personality. Until recently, there has been the universally shared problem of confinement and expectation. Cut off from the world of affairs and from a history of their own, women have turned instinctively to the present moment and to the immediate concerns of what it means to be a woman, of sometimes surrendering power in order to remain human.

But do these writers of universal themes find a universal audience? Are they taken seriously? Some years ago, a Canadian reviewer described a novel that illuminated the subject of motherhood as a *diaper novel.* With this term, he attacked not the way in which the novel was written, but more basically, the validity of the experience and its rightful place in literature. It has been a struggle for women writers to persuade themselves that their experiences are relevant. Other people who must be persuaded are the following: publishers, editors, Canada Council juries, teachers of creative writing, reviewers, booksellers, and finally, readers—those readers who sometimes shuffle their feet and apologize for the fact that they mainly read women writers.

Women writers—everywhere—share what Isak Dinesen called the "business of being a woman," those demands that cut into a woman's time. It is only, women often think, at the expense of others that they can give themselves permission to write. Listen to Katherine Mansfield writing about the early days of her relationship with John Middleton Murry: "The house seems to take up so much time.... I get frightfully impatient and want to be working.... Well, someone's got to wash dishes and get food." Washing dishes may seem a feeble whine, but the key words in Mansfield's complaint are "frightfully impatient," because impatience leads to frustration, and frustration to anger, and if we listen to Virginia Woolf, anger often creates a distortion in a work of art, robs it of wit, blurs its edges, provides nothing but a dumping ground for the emotions.

It seems to me we're at an interesting period here on the frontier. A certain amount of dumping has taken place and a certain amount of permission has been given. Women are feeling more secure in the literary world.

It could be that women are not necessarily writing better novels, but novels about the kinds of things readers are anxious to know about. Or it could be that serious women novelists are in ascendancy around the world. The novel, after all, is the one literary form whose birth took place at a time when women were, for the first time, being educated in large numbers. And women, denied the novel of action, the novel of ideas, fell heir to the novel that reflected the daily life of ordinary people. This kind of novel was once shuttled off into a corner called domestic fiction, until it was realized, and not that many years ago, that everyone, men as well as women, possess a domestic life.

Or the current interest in women's fiction could be—and I think this is more likely—because some seventy percent of those who read novels are women—so the booksellers tell us—and that these women want to hear other women's voices. Perhaps they've always wanted these voices, but we needed Simone de Beauvoir and Betty Friedan to come along and tell us we were smarter than we thought, and then Kate Millett told us—I think it was in 1970—that we didn't have to take Henry Miller seriously any longer, and what a relief that was! Women spread the word, helping each other along, and there really is—ask publishers—a network among reading women: "You've just got to read this book," they say, and often it is a book by a woman writer.

Virginia Woolf (like one of the characters in one of my novels, I have a Woolfian bias) invoked in me an impulse to be serious. And then Margaret Laurence said to me, through her writing, "Serious, yes, but watch out for earnestness." Mavis Gallant shows how it is possible to be intelligent on the page without being pedantic. Margaret Atwood, who is, I suppose, Canada's first international star, is just plain brave—she'll tackle any orthodoxy and almost always with wit. Alice Munro describes in one of her stories what real work is. It's not just housework or looking after the husband and children; my real work, the narrator says, is "wooing distant parts of myself." These distant parts, these concealed layers of existence, shame or ecstasy or whatever, are what every writer works to get to the heart of.

Part of the appeal of women writers may be the intimacy of voice. I often think how women writers sitting at their desks are speaking not to the ages or to Humankind, but to individual readers, as though those readers were in the same room, and what they are speaking of is the texture of their own lives. Women writers often seem willing to engage with vulnerability, including themselves in that vulnerability. As a woman who has elected a writing life, I am interested in writing away the invisibility of women's lives, looking at writing as an act of redemption. In order to do this, I need the companionship, the example, of other women who are writing. This makes us, in some ways, braver.

It may be that women's writing today is more aware of itself, more inclusive, less oppressed by male patronizing or erasure, less in danger of its substance falling *off* the edge. Helen Buss has questioned the missing mother in our literature, and Canadian poet and scholar Di Brandt has asked why angry women are absent from our pages. At one time women characters in fiction were expected to be resourceful and cheerful. To confront real life was to become a whining victim. As recently as 1988, one of our finest writers, Bonnie Burnard, was taken to task by *Globe and Mail* critic William French. Her book *Women of Influence* was unacceptable to Mr. French: "The melancholy tone is unrelenting," he wrote, "and we want to escape the emotionally frigid world she portrays with such power.... Burnard has undeniable talent, and the women's problems she explores in these stories undeniably exist, but I hope in her next collection, she can make me laugh, at least once."

No wonder women's books became a refuge for women readers. There they found themselves; there they could *be* themselves. There they felt the distance shrink between what was privately felt and universally known. Women, I think, were hungry for their own honesty, and both readers and writers were relieved to know that the disparagement they had suffered at the edge was undeserved. You can tell, a male critic once wrote of a beautifully cryptic Alice Munro story, just where Ms. Munro knocks off for a cup of tea.

It was Muriel Spark who broke the spell for me, finally, in a novel called *Loitering with Intent*, with her stirring sentence: "How wonderful it feels to be an artist and a woman in the twentieth century." I'd known all along it was true, but to see it bravely centred on the page made it real, and this utterance encourages me to frame a paraphrase and bring it home: how wonderful to be a woman living and writing in Canada.

In Brief . . .

- Women writers in particular may find the following in the short story form:
  - time as present and personal and urgent
  - a wider emotional range, and less exaggeration, less mythologizing
  - simple but universal settings: enclosures, rooms, houses
  - a commonality of subject matter; subject matter made accessible by being rooted in the lives of women and easily translatable from one culture to another
- The choice of the short story form may reflect that women have been cut off from the world of affairs and from a history of their own, and so have turned to the present moment and to the immediate concerns of what it means to be a woman, of sometimes surrendering power in order to remain human.
- Women readers want to read about women's lives.
- In writing, speak not to the ages or to Humankind, but to individual readers, as though those readers were in the same room.
- Be willing to engage with vulnerability, including yourself in that vulnerability.
- Now, as never before, it seems important that men and women understand each other's experience.

~ 11 ~

WRITING WHAT WE'VE DISCOVERED—SO FAR

WHEW! FOR A WHILE THERE I WORRIED ABOUT THE FUTURE OF fiction, which resembled nothing so much as an invalid thrashing and writhing on an ever narrowing bed. But the threat of other media—films, video, and particularly television—each wanting its own slice of narrative, has brought to the novel and short story a flush of health, perhaps even the beginning of a new default tradition in which the written word does what only the written word can do.

It was a close call. The patient nearly died. There was that lengthy period in which we endured a crisis of meaning so traumatic that we began to think that since words could mean anything, they could also mean nothing. Luckily, the world kept intruding, and linguistic skepticism remained a theory. Besides, only a few writers seemed able to squeeze any juice out of the thing. On the whole, postmodernism is a far too forgiving mode, and during the plague a great deal of fast-food ambiguity, in love with its own muscle tissue, passed itself off as the real thing.

Just as serious, because it came at about the same time, was the apparent exhaustion of realism, already badly nibbled away by other media that could often do it better. The old problem-solution track began to seem like a set-up, and people started asking how much realism was really in realism. The experience of women, for example, was insufficiently represented and honoured. And valued and listened to and published and read and respected. Most of what we call realistic fiction looked like a photo opportunity for catching people in crisis. Only think of that so-called realistic novel *Ordinary People*, some years back, with its wealthy families, its suicide attempts, drowning, neurosis, guilt and family breakdown. And if you think divorce statistics in our society are alarming— half of all marriages doomed—you should look up the figures in contemporary fiction. Look, too, at the angst quotient and measure it against the people you know. Look at how the historical background is shaded in—another set-up. And the way those big, heavy themes reach for the innards of folks and remind us that, listen, this is a serious book by a serious and very thoughtful writer.

People got scared, or else exasperated, and retreated for a time into a minimalism so restricted that entire novels were composed of media syntax, brand names and infantile expletives. Writers, it seemed, were always out buying cheap underwear at Sears or else they were down at the 7-Eleven, hanging out. Cynical, we lost faith in our culture and decided to diminish the language as well.

The next slightly more refined version of realism opened its arms to cliché, cliché of language and substance. I never again want to read a story that starts out: "Lily set the table with her best china and a pair of tall tapering candles. Tonight was going to be special." Reading this, or listening to it rise in my own consciousness, I also hear a second voice, whispering lewdly in my ear and saying: "Who cares." I'm not going to be bought off by mere novelty, but

I might pay a little more attention if Lily sets her table in a tent or on the 300th floor or if she invites six blind priests to dinner, or three ex-husbands or an unemployed organ grinder, or if she prepares a centrepiece of dead fish and a handful of pearls. At bottom, though, we know Lily is about to experience one of those moments when she will step forward and say: "And then I realized..." I no longer want to read about selfish, weak people whose weak, selfish marriages have come apart, and I am distrustful of those writers who can't trust their own fantasies, or who use mental aberration as the sole motivating force.

Some time ago, judging a short story competition, I was momentarily buoyed up to find a story that opened with this line: "One morning I woke up and found I had turned into a pencil." The story continued, the character admiring his nicely shaved point and bouncing along happily on his rubber eraser, but the whole thing collapsed when we were told this person was only having a nervous breakdown, and only thought he had become a pencil.

The new new new fiction—for what do you call what comes after postmodernism—seems to me to be letting in some of the particles of the world, but hanging on to the boldness and linguistic daring that the best postmodernists showed us, a new spoon of grammar stirring its bowl of words in a different way. A return to realism, yes, but a reality that is enormously expanded so that those private areas of human consciousness have found a way into our fictions. We spend, after all, nine-tenths of our lives submerged in a kind of watery silence, which is almost never reflected in literature. It gets forgotten, it gets overlooked, even while it whispers and snuffles and nags and informs us of what we share. Take the writer Nicholson Baker, who published a whole story about that weightless, helpless, surprising sensation of breaking a shoelace, how it comes flying loose in the hand—a sensation we all recognize, but when have you seen it in words, and furthermore, it can't be done on television.

We were persuaded for a while that the world was so senseless, the gap between language and meaning so wide, that we could only make our observations ironically—and most of us during that time came down with a severe case of lockjaw. As was said of Henry James, he chewed more than he bit off. But the new new new fiction does the double trick of looking ironically at irony, so that it doesn't paint itself into that cramped corner which is so sharply angled with its own cuteness that it pinches the spirit.

Characters are returning too, not those loveable, cagey eccentrics, those gruff crazy grouches, those wise-cracking waitresses who never did exist, but people who in their cortex or hearts or genitalia or hips or tongue celebrate the fact that we are all a little crazier than anyone ever thought or dared to write down. The new new new fiction lets the reader in, and—writer and reader—we live in our own creaturely dust, our own cracks in the world, thinking our unclassifiable, irreducible thoughts, and wanting now and then to sit down and talk the whole thing over and tell each other what we've discovered—so far.

In Brief . . .

The new new new fiction is characterized by

- the boldness and linguistic daring that the best post-modernists showed us
- expanded depictions of reality that include private areas of human consciousness
- looking ironically at irony
- people who celebrate the fact that we are all a little crazier than anyone ever thought or dared to write down
- the sharing of what we have discovered—so far

~ 12 ~

OPEN EVERY QUESTION, EVERY POSSIBILITY

April 8, 1996

I thought I might talk about the human need for narrative, and how our available narratives don't always match our experience. Perhaps I could call it "Narrative Hunger and the Overflowing Cupboard."

And describe it as: "High on the list of human needs, along with food, shelter, clothing, and contact, is our hunger for stories. Narrative provides us with links to the past, and the means by which to weigh our stories beside those of others, so that we can apprehend our place in the world. But for one reason or another, a large proportion of human experience fails to make the narrative record. Who do we choose to be our chroniclers, and why? What becomes of our suppressed or 'lost' stories? And how can we rescue more of the world's storyboard, so that when we open the narrative cupboard we will find enough to sustain us?"

Let me know if this will do.

—Letter from Carol Shields to Lou Hurckes, a Chicago
supporter of the arts, concerning the subject of an upcoming speech

I REMEMBER ONCE, IN PARIS, WALKING PAST A STREET PERSON, sitting on his patch of pavement with a sign around his neck that said: "*J'ai faim.*" When I saw him again an hour later he was eating an enormous ham sandwich, and it occurred to me that the sign around his neck should have been corrected to read "*J'ai eu faim.*" Here, to be sure, was a man momentarily satisfied, but conscious of further hunger to come, possibly an enlarged or existential hunger—for a coded message, a threaded notation, an orderly account or story that would serve as a witness to his place in the world.

If literature is not about the world, what is it about? *Luckily* all the world is up for sale. *Un*luckily, a good part of the world falls through the narrative sieve, washing through the fingers of the recorder's hands, and is lost. It is this simultaneous abundance and loss that I want to talk about—how, while the narrative cupboard is full to bursting, the reader is left fed, but still hungry. There is so much that lies out of reach, so much that touches only tangentially on our lives or confronts us with incomprehensible images.

Everyone recognizes that narrative hunger is a part of the human personality. Why else have our newspapers been filled with advice columns, for golden-agers, for adolescents, mid-lifers, parents, consumers, patients and professionals? It's not, I think, for the solutions that we devour this daily stream of print, but for a glimpse of human dilemma, the inaccessible stories of others.

Even the smallest narrative fragments have the power to seduce. The obituaries in our local newspaper speak of the late departed Elvira Martindale, who, besides being devoted wife *to*, beloved mother *of*, was also Manitoba Ladies' Lacrosse champion in the year 1937. Writers of film scripts would designate Elvira's victory as Plot Point A in Ms. Martindale's life-movie. What a day it must have been, what a triumph!—to be carried in the memory for fifty years! And then fifty years of anticlimax?—is that how we are to read this notice? (I used to be ashamed of reading the obituaries, and then I discovered that everyone else did too, and that they read them not only out of morbidity, but out of a natural, and I like to think healthy, longing to expand their own lives.) Here's another. John Jay Trevor, we read, has fought his affliction bravely, and, in death, asks that in lieu of flowers, friends and family send contributions to the International Society of Button and Buttonhook Collectors. On the same page: Ross and Judy McGowan of Calgary perish in a car accident after "a great day of powder skiing."

> Years ago I belonged to a small writing group, and the leader of
> our group, a woman named Gwen Reidman, advised us to read
> obituaries because they carry, like genes packed tight in their
> separate chromosomes, tiny kernels of narrative. These little
> yelps of activity—Gwen always referred to them as putty—are so
> personal and authentic and odd that they are able to reinforce the
> thin tissue of predictable fiction and bend it into unlikely shapes.
>
> —*Unless*

Telephone companies have learned to pitch their TV ads in emotional narrative context. You've all seen them: the tense lonely father anxious to hear whether his son has passed his bar exam. An elderly woman awaiting news of the birth of her granddaughter. These are weepies, little melodramas, bad art perhaps, but packaged like appetizers, hors d'œuvres, to appease our narrative hunger.

The manufacturers of Dewar's Scotch Whisky know how much we need the seeds of stories and how we need, too, to place our own stories beside those of others, to compare, weigh, judge and forgive, and to find an angle of vision that renews our image of where *we* are in the world. Their advertisements, usually on the back covers of slick magazines, profile the beautiful and rich, telling us when and how they made their first million, what book they are presently reading, what is their favourite meal, their favourite restaurant, and of course, favourite drink, their philosophy for success—the same life-bites, in fact, that novelists seize upon.

Family video adventures. Anecdotes swapped at lunch or overhead on a bus, sidewalk, café. Newspaper fillers: an item in the *Globe and Mail*, for instance, noting the fact that thirteen people are killed annually in North America by overturned vending machines—a narrative nugget I was able to use in a novel.

TV sitcoms. Song lyrics. Jokes. Urban myths. Comic strips. Such a wealth of material to draw on, but never... quite... enough. And never quite accurate either, *glancing off* the epic of human experience rather than reflecting it back to us. And provoking, at the same time, that contradiction: that narrative hunger is very often a perverse pleasure to the overfed.

We may not know exactly what a novel is, but there are certain characteristics of the novel as we know it and write it—that is, the novel that went off like a firecracker in 1740 and that continues to be, in our society anyway, the literary form of choice. Some of these characteristics include: 1. A texture that approximates the world as we know it; 2. Characters who in their struggles with the world resemble ourselves; 3. Dilemmas that remind us of our own predicaments; 4. Scenes that trigger our memories or tap into our yearnings; and 5. Conclusions that shorten the distance between what is privately felt and universally known, so that we look up from the printed page and say, "Aha!"

But how relevant *are* these definition points, and how close to our lives have our narratives *ever* come?

We can start, maybe, with the admission that both real events and their accompanying narratives are conveyed to us by words, and that words, words alone, will always fail in their attempt to express what we mean by reality. We cannot think without words—or so many believe—and thus the only defence against words is more words. But we need to remember that the labyrinth of language stands *beside* reality itself, a somewhat awkward, almost always distorted facsimile or matrix. Experience, reality that is, possesses immediacy; language plods behind, a rational or irrational tortoise. It may take pages of print to reproduce a registered vision, a shooting star, an uplifted ocean wave, an uplifted eyebrow even. What if we were to estimate that half of felt experience falls away in our efforts to describe or contain or conserve a moment in time? If you were to imagine that a circle represents the well-stocked narrative cupboard, and that it is diminished by that estimate, we can cut our circle down by half.

Think of the naïve tourist who records in his diary a description of the crier in a mosque, believing he would recall with his written artifact the notes of the call to prayer. Language that is so useful in the province of the intellect is a relatively clumsy vehicle in the expression of emotion and narrative movement. Even the finest brush strokes of Henry James, or Marcel Proust or Alice Munro are dabs in the darkness. The weightiest, most detailed description of the storming of the Bastille—to take an instance—forms a papery, speculative rustle beside the actual event. Reality smells better than words, tastes sharper, presses on the skin more compellingly.

"Writing is mere writing," Annie Dillard says, and "literature is mere." "An ordinary reader picking up a book," she says, "can't yet hear a thing; it will take half an hour to pick up the writing's modulations, its ups and downs and louds and softs." Every unwinding story relies on language parts, its only assigned building material, to give it permanence and shape.

I hope I can begin with this shared notion: that both "reality" and literature are joined in the need for language and that they labour under the crippling limitations that language imposes. And I hope you'll agree with me, too, that language is not disinterested, that it flows from a bank of cultural references, both private and shared. It flows with purpose, with, shall we say, an agenda. The crier in the minaret has an agenda too, no doubt, but the man jotting his notes into his travel journal, or perhaps pulling out his video camera, is moved by completely other forces.

Narrative that questions experience, repositions experience, expands or contracts experience, rearranges experience, dramatizes experience, and which brings, without apology: colour, interpretation and political selection, has been with us since the earliest stirrings of the human tongue. The primal narratives are believed—though how can we be sure?—to be accounts of fallen heroes or adventures of the hunt. Imagine a small colony of an early culture, then, seated around a fire and discussing the capture of, say, a male bison. Someone will begin the tale; but who is that someone and how has he been selected? Is it because he captures the details accurately or because he is able to speak vividly? I'm using the "he" pronoun deliberately, since it was mainly male narrated stories that entered the literature before the eighteenth century.

Even as late as 1957, Northrup Frye, that good and humane scholar, was able to announce, authoritatively, that there are precisely four forms of fiction. (This, by the way, may have been the last time in our history that such definitive summations were possible.) Frye lists dozens of male fiction writers (and one woman named George and another named Jane), a disproportion of writers and of women's experience that radically diminishes the narrative pool, making it look something like our imaginary circle halved once again.

But I'd like to return for a minute to the primitive storyteller relating the story of the hunt. Does he know the value of a narrative pause? Does he know how to lead up to the bison's death, how to keep his audience waiting, how to bring a scene into focus by a telling detail or by the use of metaphor? Is he able to release himself from the tyranny of authenticity and, with the full complicity of his listeners, heighten his narrative with a small exaggeration, perhaps even a gross exaggeration, perhaps even the breaking of an important sequence, or the insertion of an invented incident or character, or the substitution of one event for another? Perhaps he'll turn the male bison into a female, give it an extra horn or a set of wings. What if the storyteller had never seen a bison, what if the hunting grounds had lost their promise and nothing remained but an old inherited narrative of the storyteller's forebears—would he be forced to relinquish his place around the fire, would he be silenced, mocked for his distortions and inventions and roughly dismissed? Or would he find a place of honour in his society, a society that admitted, openly or tacitly, that our own lives are never quite enough for us, and that had a hunger for narrative, for storytelling that is probably about 40,000 years old.

And yet, we continue, even today, to be troubled by a perceived dichotomy between what is called "reality" and what is known as fiction. This sorting out of "reality"—those quote marks again—and invention is not a new problem, but a very old one, and it has to do, I think, with the inability of fiction to stare at itself. So many questions arise. Is there such a thing as truth? Can we set aside our attachment to honesty? Who makes the rules? Who is telling the story, and how does the teller relate to the tale? Exactly how far can a teller take a tale? Can a fiction writer, for instance, write about a year that is 400 days long? About daisies that fall from the sky instead of rain? (You will recognize this particular event from García Márquez's *One Hundred Years of Solitude.* Now there's a man who knows how to bend and rattle the narrative apparatus.) Can the novelist rename a street in Winnipeg (I got into all sorts of trouble when I did) or make a cat fly? Do we accept the fact that fiction is not strictly mimetic, that we want it to spring *out* of the world, *illuminate* the world, not mirror it back to us?

Yes, you will say, or perhaps no, and your response will depend on the culture you live in, the era into which you are born, and on the width or narrowness of your aesthetic or moral responses. Huge pieces of potential narrative have been sacrificed in the name of authenticity, of not telling the untrue, not risking deviance. (We can snip our circle again.) Here I can only estimate the size of the loss.

"Reality" has generally held on to its authority, at least until recently, but fiction, it seems, has been defending itself forever.

Either that or finding sly wink-of-the-eye ways to circumvent moral skepticism. The "stories" that take their roots in mythology or in our scriptures establish their legitimacy by their divine origins or ethical purpose. The novels of Danielle Steel demand their way by promising a light diversion from the serious problems that trouble us. Sadly, narratives without a ticket don't get on the train.

Enormous quantities of stories, perhaps the finest stories of our culture, have been lost through illiteracy or lack of permission, either a prohibition placed on the storyteller, most often "Women, hold thy tongue" (a snip again, again dividing our circle) or the simple inability to write down one's experience on paper (snip). The historian Theodore Zeldin, who has written with such thoroughness about the civilization of France, tells us that, in the tenth century, nine-tenths of the French were peasants. And yet, we possess only one personal eyewitness account of French peasant life in that century, and even that account must be looked at with some skepticism, since its author became literate eventually and left his peasant past behind, skewing the sample. There are, however, dozens of novels set in the rural France of that period, novels whose authors have leapt across the synapse of what is known and what is imagined, or have deduced their historic narratives from artifacts, paintings or documents. Do at least some of them get it right? An unanswerable question. And an unfair question, perhaps. Is conjecture better than nothing at all when it comes to reaching into the narrative cupboard for something to eat?

Humankind cannot bear very much reality, T. S. Eliot once said. (Snip.) Happy stories are doomed to extinction, says Lorrie Moore. (Snip.) We will never have a true account of war, said novelist

John Hersey. No one could bear to write it. No one could bear to read it. (Snip.) The world would split open if one woman told the truth, says poet Muriel Rukeyser. (Snip.)

And then there are the stories that are excavated authentically enough from the past, but lose their meaning to contemporary sensibility. You may be familiar with Robert Darnton's book *The Great Cat Massacre*, in which a famous eighteenth-century joke is examined in order to see what light it throws on French society of that time, and the way people thought during the Enlightenment. We are introduced to a cat-loving master printer in Paris. His young and unruly apprentices kill his dozen or so cats one night and string them up in the print shop for the master to discover in the morning. *That is the joke*, a joke that travelled across Europe over a period of several years and apparently cracked up the populace. The cat massacre joke has been carefully analyzed for historical context, for language puns, looked at from every possible perspective, but its humour remains stubbornly opaque, even alarming: something is askew here, either in the narrative, or with the society that delighted in it, or—could it possibly be?—with us? (Snip).

Another problem: Since the days of relating stories of the hunt around the fire we've grown self-conscious about our fictions, inventing categories—tragedy and comedy, after all, are only a convenient and arbitrary shorthand, a crude approximation—and we've made rules about how stories must be shaped. Rules about unity of time and space, about conflict, rising action and the nature of story conclusions. Our narratives, then, have had their hair cut and permed; they've been sent to the fat farm where they've learned to take nano-bites out of their own flesh in order to maintain a sleek literary line, a line that will assign itself to one of those major genres or else surrender to deconstructive surgery, and disconnect, more and more, from the texture and rhythm of "reality."

For a life, as writer Sandra Gulland reminds us, does not unfold in chapters—you may have noticed this. A life does not have an underlying theme, yet we seem to believe a novel must. A life does not build slowly but steadily to a climax. A life is rarely restricted to three main characters. In life, a new character may enter the scheme in the final pages, but in fiction we have declared this an offence against aesthetic order. And so, ungainly or overweight stories fall out of the narrative record (snip); they're too bulgy for theory, too untidy for analysis. Too hard to teach. In or out of the official canon, stories really are described as being teachable or not, and you can imagine what happens to those that are deemed unteachable. (Snip.)

Contemporary stories may be very different from the old tale of the bison hunt, but the long history of the teller and the tale does offer up a remarkably persistent pattern, what critics such as Robert Alter call "deep structures." We can go straight to *Ulysses* to see an early model: the tale of the wanderer, the homeless, the picaresque hero with an unsteady eye, an inability to effect change, a being helplessly adrift. Often orphaned, spiritually or else psychologically, and often wounded, maimed in some way, either metaphorically or otherwise, the picaresque traveller is someone who stands outside of events, who, in fact, chooses that position.

If the outsider is the most persistent of literary heroes in our tradition, we can probably conclude that those who elect themselves writers are also outsiders. What then happens to the narratives that arise at the centre of our society and to the point of view of those who choose to stay rooted at that centre? Are they lost? (Snip.)

Are these narratives erased from the collective memory as well as the literary storehouse? If so, what an enormous gap there must be between the nexus of life and the literature that grows on its margins. You can see the predicament this puts us in: society invites its outsiders to keep the narrative record, to select and shape those stories that will survive in the culture.

In our view of narrative, we eliminate, cut off (snip) an immense slice of the world's story horde, those stories possessing the brevity and shape of a Zen koan, or stories such as those we find in, say, the Cree tradition, that refuse to complete themselves according to the narrative arc our culture has sanctioned.

Even within our own culture, certain narrative material leaks away for want of a catchment vessel. I'm told by my linguistic friends that English is poor in words that describe mystical or transcendental experiences, and there is a well known and bitterly chilling story about a New England housewife who, when washing dishes one evening, happened to notice how the soap bubbles gathered in a wreath around her wrist, and how the fading light from the window picked up a thousand tiny rainbows. She found the moment beautiful and profound, and seemed to sense in the apparition something of the order and meaning of the universe. Excited, she called her husband and attempted to share the vision with him. He immediately sent for on ambulance and had her transferred to a mental hospital. (Snip.)

We speak, too, of the absent narratives, the negative element of a photographic print—the dark void or unbridgeable gap, shadows, and mirages, the vivid dream that fades by morning, the missed bus, the men we didn't marry, the unconceived child, the confession murmured to a priest, or *not* murmured to a priest. The pockets of time and light that are too evanescent to be put into words or even to catch the eye. This narrative lint refuses to collect itself, and is lost to our memory and to the narrative record. (Snip.)

I recently read a book called *Ruby: An Ordinary Woman*, made up of the diary extracts of one Ruby Alice Side Thompson—so ordinary a woman that you will not recognize her name. The diaries span the years 1909 to 1969. The entries are selected from forty-two handwritten notebooks that were doomed to obscurity, when, entirely by accident, they were rescued by a granddaughter and put into print. How many other such accounts go to the dump? (Snip.) Accounts that, like Ruby's, would change forever the way we think of women's lives during that period?

Our stories distort the past, then; probably no one ever thought otherwise. Futuristic stories have always, for some reason, been relatively few in number, tinged with the exotic, and often politically weighted. What then of the stories of the moment; do they possess the midnight shine of verisimilitude, can we trust them to give a portrait or a sense of meaning to the present or even to tell us what people do and think when they are alone in a room?

In recent years, the spectre of political correctness has touched all of us, placing limits on our available narrative field, restraining even the possibilities of observation, let alone development. Political correctness, of course, has suppressed great widths of life in the past—almost all of gay society, the larger part of women's sexuality, also Catholics, Protestants, disbelievers—each taking their turn on the absentee list. (Snip.)

There are curious deformations in our stories of the present day, too. I'll address myself to just one small domestic area, the question of marriage and divorce in our society. Look into the other-world of the contemporary novel, and we find the divorce curve running wildly above the 50 percent rate of contemporary marital breakdown.

Jane Austen shows us attitudes toward marriage in her society, the search for a life partner, the developing notion of a marriage of friendship, but ask yourself when you last read a contemporary literary novel about happily married people. For one reason or another, enduring marriages (that other 50 percent of the statistical pattern) find little space on the printed page. How is a novelist to pump the necessary tension into the lives of the happily committed? Even the suggestion of a sound marital relationship posits the suspicion of what is being hidden and about to be revealed in a forthcoming chapter. Couples who have good sex, who discuss and resolve their differences, and care deeply about their bonds of loyalty are clearly as simple-minded and unimaginative as their creator. There they sit with their hobbies and their wallpaper and their cups of filtered coffee, finishing each other's sentences and nodding agreement. She sends his winter coat to the cleaners and worries about his asthma. He continues to find her aging body erotic and he's also extremely fond of her way with grilled peppers. This is all very well, but what can be done with folks so narratively unpromising? (Snip.)

It might be thought that novelists would come running forward to pick up the gauntlet. Six hundred fast-turning pages without a single marital breakdown; now there is a challenge. Two people meet, fall in love, and integrate their histories. Crises arrive, but the marriage holds firm. Really? Who would expect readers to believe this fairy tale?

Why do today's novelists distort the state of marriage by concentrating on connubial disarray? To this I can only cry *mea culpa*, since my novels and short stories are as filled with divorce as any other writer's.

I would, though, *like* to redress this rather small and curious distortion, to see more marital equity in the pages of our narratives. And I'd be willing to honour the principle of mimesis and settle for a straight 50 percent success/failure rate. Coupledom, especially when seen in an unsparing light, should not necessarily equal boredom, should it? It might be interesting to see novelists look inside their own specific human packaging and admit that a long relationship—the union of two souls, the merging of contraries, whatever—can be as complex, as potentially dynamic and as open to catharsis as the most shattering divorce.

Perhaps it is this notion of conflict that needs revisiting. It might be a project for the narratives to come, asking why the rub of disunity strikes larger sparks than the rewards of accommodation, and how we've come to privilege what separates us above that which brings us together.

Our narrative cupboard is far from being bare (snip) but it seems it needs restocking. We need perhaps to turn back to that twilight of the gods where our stories were born. And to look ahead to narrative's full potential, that bountiful human impulse that says: Once upon a time—opening every question, every possibility.

Looking at writing in Canada, the storyboard does seem to be growing here rather than shrinking. Voices formerly at the margin are now being heard, bringing with them their different rhythms and their alternate expectations. More is permitted; more can be said.

Women's writing has already begun to dismantle the rigidities of genre, those "four basic types of fiction" referred to earlier, and to replace that oppressive narrative arc we've lived with so long, the line of rising action. The definition of the real has expanded or, as writer Russell Hoban says, the bricks are falling out of the tower, letting the craziness in. Film, which conveys narratives of action superbly, has left to the written word, by default perhaps, what many of us value most in narrative: the interior voice reflecting, thinking, connecting, ticking, bringing forward a view of a previously locked room, and, to quote John Donne, making one little room an everywhere.

In Brief . . .

- We are hungry for narrative, for stories that serve as witness to our place in the world.
- Although all the world is available for narrative, much of it falls through the narrative sieve and is lost.
- There are certain characteristics of the novel as we know it and write it:
  - a texture that approximates the world as we know it
  - characters who in their struggles with the world resemble ourselves
  - dilemmas that remind us of our own predicaments
  - scenes that trigger our memories or tap into our yearnings
  - conclusions that shorten the distance between what is privately felt and universally known, so that we look up from the printed page and say, "Aha!"

~ *13* ~

WRITING FROM THE EDGE

CANADIAN WRITING IS IN A STATE OF EXUBERANT GOOD HEALTH. Why is this, you ask, and why now? There are some who believe that the perceived lack of national identity, of cultural cohesiveness, is a vacuum crying to be filled, and that the sudden burst of new writing clusters around the impulse to identify, define, and make solid what in the past has been random and unnamable. If this is true, I am sure it is unconscious, since I can't imagine a writer sitting down at her computer and thinking: Now I am going to contribute to the nexus of Canadian identity.

There are those who suggest that the Canadian literary body is so new and so loose and uncodified that writers are relatively free and unshackled to pursue their literary track. You'll remember what Robertson Davies said, how we in Canada are the attic of North America, suggesting that there's plenty of room in that dark and empty attic to shout.

I am a little reluctant to admit that we may still be colonialist enough in our posture to measure our literary health by the international stamp of approval. And so we at home notice when

Canadians appear on the Booker shortlist. And when the *New York Times'* annual list of most important books includes books by Canadians, as it did in 1996, when two were by Canadian women, Mavis Gallant and Alice Munro. I was delighted with this recognition of our two major writers, but even more pleased that at home we took the *New York Times* fairly calmly, a sign that these kinds of triumphs have become (almost) taken for granted. In addition, our recent Governor General's Award and Giller shortlists have been rich in strong and innovative fiction, and—here I go again—these novels are finding international publishers.

Simultaneous waves of fiction are coming out of the rest of the post-colonial world: India, Australia, New Zealand, the West Indies, Africa. The children have grown up, and are producing their fresh, lively, self-confident, sometimes audacious novels, beamed from parts of the world that had been for so long silent, humble, dependent, and distrustful of their own surfaces. This new writing, not *very* new when you get down to dates—Patrick White, V. S. Naipaul, our own Alice Munro—was coming from cultures not, perhaps, perfectly understood by the British reading public, coming, in fact, from the exotic margins of the planet, the far edge.

I've already mentioned the idea that the short story is, mainly, a new world form. Reports from the frontier, Hortense Calisher called them, a lovely and accurate phrase that caught my attention. Perhaps this is what all of literature is: a dispatch from the frontier, news from the edge. Even given that the edges and centres of society are forever shifting, it does seem to me that the view from the edge offers a privileged perspective. Also freedom from cynicism, if not from anger. Also a kind of real or willed innocence, which is what I believe every writer must keep alive in order to write.

As it happens, I'm somewhat acquainted with what it feels like to be on the edge. I lived for a long time in Winnipeg, a large city, but certainly not the literary centre of Canada. Though I was born in the centre of the United States, it was clear that Midwesterners were, culturally, at the edge—only remember that famous *New Yorker* cover map of the United States as viewed from Manhattan. And also at the edge, in a sense, were members of the middle class— and this is a nice irony, the middle being nowhere near the centre.

This question of edge, though, is problematic, for we have to ask ourselves how the centre is defined—and there are many centres. There is a centre we think of as the core literature or canon of the Western World, of our North American culture, of the women's tradition, but we see that more and more of that core is subject to rapid meltdown or at the very least revision. Then there is the divide between the dominant culture and the marginal culture. The early settlers and the later settlers. High culture and popular culture. And there are geographic or political entities that, for historical reasons, remained detached, isolated, or else colonized, and where a national literature is slow to flourish or else develops into a sort of sacred amber pellet imprisoned in what is believed to be the national ethos.

Having lived in Chicago, Toronto, Ottawa, Manchester, and Vancouver, I began to perceive myself as a placeless person, and naturally I wondered if this would affect my impulse to write. It didn't. I soon realized that writers, even in Manitoba, spend most of their time sitting in little rooms with the doors closed, and that it mattered very little where they were as long as there was a place in their heads that could be tagged as legitimate territory.

—*"As for Me and My House"*

A Hungarian friend told me that, at the time he left Hungary in the late fifties—and I'm sure this has changed today—the national literature was so small, and at the same time so widely disseminated, that anyone who possessed a high school education was, *ipso facto*, familiar with the entire range of Hungarian prose, drama, and poetry.

Part of me yearns for that degree of cultural saturation, a whole tradition compacted like a gemstone. Only imagine meeting strangers—on the street corner, in a bus or café, or at a private home—and finding that every cultural moment is secured, *and* refracted and enlarged, by common references, quotations, allusions, nuances, a body, in fact, of shared belief.

Another part of me would resent deeply unity of this order. To be defined by a culture as tight and total as this is surely to be confined, and to be handed at the cradle the height, width, and depth of a national literature and all the conduits of connections therein, all the orthodoxies of genre and gender, the petrification of canon, the cross-network of influences—*to know it all* would be to confess oneself part of a moribund culture. And then, to go one step further—cementing literature belly-to-belly to the national density so that every variation is suspect, is threatening, is minor or anomalous or marginal or subversive or condemned to that variant stream we call, sometimes with reverence, other times with a rolling of the eyeballs—experimental. In other words, to make the centre so unassailable that the edges are hushed into silence.

I'm more at ease with the rich variables of a randomly evoked, organically spilling, unself-conscious, disorderly, unruly, uncharted and unchartable pouring out of voice. These various surreal juxtapositions of life and literature, of time and place, of reader and writer seem to me to erase or blur national labels while, ironically, sharpening the particularities of the texts: figure against ground, ground illuminating figure, and contribution to my skepticism on the shape and force of a national literature. How fluid is it? Who gets to name it? Who gets to enter?

And Canadians, these days, are directing serious attention to that very seething, smoking, chaotic multicultural muddle that is, in fact, our reality. This is risky; one almost wants to whisper: un-Canadian.

Many of these works aren't in the canon, which must now be redressed or demolished; some aren't even in print. They are in an almost literal sense reports from the frontier, and the frontier has been shifting in recent years—in terms of geography, demography, gender, and certainly literary form. There are some curious lags: we have been for some time an urbanized society, but our literature has not, until recent years, noticed this fact, perhaps because most writers are one generation from the farm, from the frontier itself. Similarly, immigrant writers—Rohinton Mistry comes to mind—continue to write about their old countries rather than the Canada they immigrated to. It is difficult in today's Canada to locate the mainstream, the centre. It seems we are almost all at the edge, and that edge embraces aboriginal writing, gay writing, immigrant writing, and women's writing.

It may be the noisy and varied writing coming out of Canada today that makes it difficult to compare that literature with that of the United States, but I don't think such a comparison has *ever* been easy. It has been suggested that Canadian writing, reflecting the immigration patterns of the country, is more community centred while American writing focuses on the individual, the

Canadian *who are we* rather than the American *who am I*, but this is extremely difficult to prove. Canadian writing is more sombre, it's said, more modest, more self-deprecating, more moderate in its ambitions, but again, novel for novel, this is not easily demonstrated. What we can say with certainty is that Canadian literature is smaller than American literature and younger. There are nineteenth-century Canadian novels, to be sure, but not many and no great novels from that century. We can, speaking roughly and without stepping on too many toes, take the year 1960 as the real beginning of our literature. That was the year—just to peg it for you—when there were five Canadian novels published in English in Canada. Five!

Today's refocusing or defocusing of Canadian literature may be a reaction to our experience in the sixties, the time of our centenary, and the years that followed, a period of explosive patriotism, partly genuine, partly pumped-up boosterism, when we were persuaded to rush our literary impulses into a unified statement of national identity. We had a railway, an airline, a new flag, an anthem—why not a literature too?

Many Canadians think now with embarrassment of this period, but most believe it was a necessary process. Extravagant claims were made for rather mediocre old texts—and for me the novels of Frederick Philip Grove are out on the marginal edge of the edge—and far too many new novels, volumes of poetry and plays were brought forward and celebrated simply because they contained—and this was and continues to be a catch phrase—Canadian content. Because we needed a critical language to talk about the new Canadian writing, theories were hastily concocted and eagerly taken up. These cobbled together theories became hobbling tyrants.

The idea of the garrison mentality, for instance, which poor Northrop Frye mentioned only once and only in passing, became a verity, until it was, finally, demolished when revisionists began to pay attention to what our nineteenth century writers had really said about nature and society.

None of this is surprising, perhaps, in a post-colonial country where writers had long been persuaded that life, real life, happened elsewhere. Susanna Moodie set her rather lugubrious novels in England, and in an England that had long since vanished. Hugh MacLennan was driven to despair trying to interest American publishers in his Canada-based novels. As recently as the 1930s and '40s, Morley Callaghan published some of his novels in double editions: a Toronto setting for those books sold in Canada, a Chicago setting for those sold south of the border. Gabrielle Roy wrote in her autobiography that, as a young Franco-Manitoban writer, she grew conscious of what she calls a worm in the apple, the feeling that she was so doubly at the edge that she belonged nowhere. And what can we say about a country whose bookstores still, today, divide their offerings into Literature and—a very small shelf usually—Canadiana; that's where our novels appear side by side with manuals about how to master white-water canoeing.

Nations are fortunate indeed if they possess texts—*Huckleberry Finn* comes to mind—whose spirit is universally shared—well, almost—and understood even by those who have never read them and never will. *David Copperfield* is, for Britain, a similar cultural key; touch that key and you stir directly into the available culture. We may not yet have in Canada such a universally shared cultural reference, though the name Hagar Shipley from Margaret Laurence's *The Stone Angel* goes a long way in that direction.

When Margaret Laurence said to Canadian writers if you can nail down one piece of this strange country, then you have an obligation to do it, she almost certainly was signalling that well known irony: that radical regionalism often produces universal response. People are bonded and nourished by a common literature, but only if it has flowered naturally, unprodded by politicians and flag wavers and the prescriptive notions of the Academy.

In 1957, I crossed the border with my young husband, all our belongings, including an ironing board, packed into our six-cylinder Ford. This was the year of the founding of the Canada Council. It was decided by a number of concerned citizens, and with the blessing of Parliament, and with the help of a substantial and timely private endowment, that Canada, this country on the edge, could afford its own culture.

We had at that time only a handful of novelists. Our literature, in fact, was probably a good deal smaller than that of Hungary, and there were probably only a few names—Leacock, Callaghan—who were part of the public currency. Pierre Berton had just begun his explorations; Juliette sang from the radio, and the Happy Gang did their gig every day right after the Farm Report.

After 1957, perhaps because of the thrust of the Canada Council, or perhaps because it was time, regional theatres and symphonies sprang to life across the country. Art galleries mounted Canadian shows. Plays were produced that were written by Canadian playwrights; this had scarcely ever happened before. And librarians from Newfoundland to Vancouver Island began pasting those little red maple leafs on the spines of Canadian books, although I have to say that writers, even today, are uncertain about whether they applaud this distinction or not; certainly I can't imagine Americans attaching the Stars and Stripes to *their* books.

It wasn't until the middle 1960s that I read my first Canadian novel, which happened to be Marian Engel's *The Honeyman Festival.* Of course I'd seen Leonard Cohen and Irving Layton doing their *shtick* on television, so I knew there was some literary activity going on. The next novel I read was Margaret Laurence's *The Stone Angel,* and one year after that, I found myself registering for a graduate degree in Canadian Literature at the University of Ottawa and beginning preliminary research on the Canadian pioneer Susanna Moodie.

Both Marian Engel and Margaret Laurence were young mothers when they wrote their wonderful books, and they were assisted in their work by grants from the Canada Council that enabled them to "buy" time. I don't believe for a minute that we can produce writers by throwing money at them, but the Canada Council has, from the beginning, established a climate of respect for the arts and those who practise them. Writers could be nourished both directly and indirectly, given financial support and awarded social permission to create novels that were wrenched out of the lives of Canadians. It was a gamble and it took time—though a surprisingly short time—and what we have today—our own literature—is as indebted to the Canada Council, as well as provincial arts councils, as it is to Canada's position "on the edge."

In Brief . . .

- Canadian writers should contribute to a randomly evoked, organically spilling, unself-conscious, disorderly, unruly, uncharted and unchartable pouring out of voice.
- You can blur national labels while sharpening particularities; radical regionalism often produces a universal response.

~ *14* ~

BE BOLD ALL THE WAY THROUGH

JOURNALING PAYS. KEEP SEPARATE ONES FOR THINGS YOU SEE, the beginnings of stories, what catches your attention. Use it to learn how to write sentences; practise in a journal.

Recognize clichés. Don't use them or clichéd ideas, e.g., "All people in an asylum are sane; we're the ones who are insane."

Set a structure. Sit and write a certain amount of time. Have a place to go and sit.

Rituals are useful. You need time around the time to write, to get into the fictional world.

Try to write two pages a day. Do your two pages, then go for a walk. Think about what you've written and where it will go organically the next day.

Read what you wrote the previous day to enter the other reality.

Read one page of the dictionary to settle your mind.

Don't write yourself out; write to the point of exhaustion, not past it. Save something to prime the pump the next day.

Structure comes out of content, not the reverse.

For character and plot development, don't think it out, but let them evolve organically so that their growth is nurtured. Trust the first draft to develop into something thick.

A story is something moving to someone else. That is all.

There is one line that unwinds a poem. A poem should be a flash of a camera; some part of it goes off.

The idea of rhyme in poetry comes out of prayer, incantations, ringing bell, hands clapping.

Poetry hands people an experience they've had but haven't articulated.

For Gary Geddes, poems are little toys he carries around in his head.

In poetry, avoid commenting on images you create.

Use a thesaurus.

After writing, ask yourself, "Is this what I really mean?"

Every writer is troubled with getting what's in the head onto paper.

How to move an image forward: Ask yourself, what is the worst thing that could happen to this set-up? Have the telephone ring (plays). Have several obstacles, a range of them, to drive new narrative ideas.

Some narratives move very slowly. Let them move at their pace.

How to find the essential idea, something to write about: 1. Write down ideas, brilliant ones do slip away. 2. Who am I—self-discovery. 3. We always see narrative scraps around us to be filled out.

Have faith in your own material, what passionately interests you. Felt passion makes it interesting.

> I have no idea what will happen in this book. It is a mere
> abstraction at the moment, something that's popped out of the
> ground like the rounded snout of a crocus on a cold lawn. I've
> stumbled against this idea in my clumsy manner, and now the urge
> to write it won't go away. This will be a book about lost children,
> about goodness, and going home and being happy and trying to
> keep the poison of the printed page in perspective. I'm desperate
> to know how the story will turn out.
>
> —*Unless*

Alice Munro takes a simple narrative structure and gives it fullness. Learn from her. Reading her is as good as taking a creative writing course.

Language is the most interesting, generating vocabulary, letting it flow. Let language flow out.

Let yourself be as crazy as possible.

Use what you know. Alice Munro hires a researcher.

Everyone says the first sentence is the most important, but the truth is the second one is.

Going from one place to another is hard. Don't use "meanwhile."

Get rid of "just," "very," "somehow," and "would" (which is dead wood) and "there" at the beginning of a sentence. Replace "all of a sudden" and "suddenly" with nothing or with "then" or "but then."

You don't have to write every step the characters take. "An hour later" is sufficient.

Leave an opening in writing; don't paint yourself into a corner.

Write long sentences branched at both ends and balance them with short ones. When you've finished a paragraph, look at the beginning of the sentences to see that they don't all start the same way.

Don't worry about writing autobiographically out of fear of injuring others. First write everything about the person accurately, and mask it later. One can alter components of a piece after writing it. Robertson Davies, when asked why he was writing so well into his sixties said: "People died."

How to give structure to so many lives? The answer is that everything, life, keeps going.

The discovery that privately held experiences are real, this is what literature is about. We're not alone.

Alice Munro often transposes into past and present tense, back and forth, an effective way to get the best of both worlds. Use the present tense for a sense of immediacy. In Margaret Laurence's *Diviners* the chapters change tense in a pattern.

On appropriation of voice: You should be able to write about anything you chose. We need to go outside our own skins. The problems come when experience is falsely conveyed without accuracy and respect.

Don't put undue faith in the idea of conflict in story. That shape, like an upside-down V, is not real anymore. The new audience wants a love of text, character. Alice Munro is interested in the impulse of murder rather than who did it. You should be aware of the lives of characters, what they do, outside the story.

E. M. Forster acknowledged that in any narrative there will be characters to be rounded and others who are flat; this is a convention we accept.

Endings can simply go off spiralling.

Although most good writing is done alone (and don't for this reason take too many courses) consider collaborative writing, writing in a community instead of in isolation. A play in particular lends itself to collaboration. Work with someone who has the same idea of schedule and workload, but is different from you.

One of our collaborators is the economy—plays, for one example, are formed by the amount of money available for actors, staging.

Use clichés as comforting murmurs—comforting to the characters.

It is *hard* to take sentences out.

Be bold *all the way through*—keep the reader's attention.

People like to read dialogue. This is a way to provide the relationships between people and information about age, class, gender, what they do without spelling it out. Dialogue can give tone to your writing and keep it transparent. Say your dialogue out loud so that it sounds natural.

Use lots of contractions and don't be afraid of using "said." You can paragraph each new speaker with "he said," "she said." Put "she said" in the middle of long dialogue, not at the end.

The best way to introduce yourself to the basis of storytelling is through fairy tales and the Old Testament. Storytelling reminds you to use freedom in story—to jump into it.

"I can see it." This must happen or the manuscript is dead.

Finding a voice can take lots of false tries. It takes time to settle into it. If you are lucky, things arrive in the passage of time. Once you find it, stay faithful to a voice.

Writing is going the way of film—quick cuts. Paragraphing can move you easily, and is a good tool. Mavis Gallant often has one-sentence paragraphs.

Be careful about using dreams—they are fascinating to the dreamer only.

If you use flashbacks, there must be more than one, each must be of a similar length, and there must be a pattern of how they work out.

Description is the right detail in the right place. Don't present details in lists; keep the reader's patience in mind.

Style is a sum of the choices you've made. You don't need to back off from telling why you're changing style, but changing style needs transitions.

A playwright must include the audience in a web of enchantment.

A play must have a "through line"—a term dramatists use. I think an audience needs a person, not just a theme or motif. I can say this after seeing three plays in one week, only one of which had enough epoxy to hold it together. Oddly enough, though, even seeing bad plays is instructive when in the act of writing one. You can see what is possible.

In the short postcard story form (a story that would fit on a post-card) the concentration is on tiny details, miniatures, and then the immense, in surprising ways. Sudden fiction is like postcard stories.

When you use a bank of cultural references, you know you'll miss some people.

FROM THE LETTERS

CAROL KEPT UP CORRESPONDENCE WITH HUNDREDS OF FRIENDS, readers, colleagues and others. Many of the letters she exchanged with the writer Blanche Howard have been collected in a 2007 book published by Viking Canada, *A Memoir of Friendship: The Letters between Carol Shields and Blanche Howard*, edited by Blanche and her daughter Allison Howard. The first letter in that book is from Carol to Blanche, writing from Saint-Quay-Portrieux, France, where our family was spending a sabbatical year. At that time, Carol had published two books of poetry but had yet to establish her career as a novelist. This first letter evokes the questions often heard from writers who have just had their first book accepted and who want to know more about contracts, copyright, advances and the like.

August 6, 1975
St. Quay-Portrieux, France
Dear Blanche:

I am writing to you for some advice; I've finally finished the novel I was writing and finally (after being turned down three times) found a publisher for it. The contract arrived yesterday and, although everything looks fine, we haven't the least idea about such things. Don had the happy idea of writing to you—which pleased me since I've been wanting to write to you anyway—and seeing what you think. I know you aren't a lawyer, but you have been through this and may have some ideas. If you do I would love to hear from you.

Blanche wrote back with sound advice—the contract seemed standard and "was probably adequate." This was the start of several decades of thoughts on deeper, broader topics: writing, the meaning of life, reading, politics, family, self.

In later years my mother sent letters of advice to her students at the writing program at Humber College, Toronto, and to many others, including me when I began to write columns and stories. She was a keen advocate of writing as a vocation, telling me, in a letter dated May 27, 1987 (when I was about to set off to live for a year in England and Italy), "I can't tell you how fortunate I feel to have this portable profession, and I always wonder how other people manage."

We had written a story together, published in 1985 in my mother's collection *Various Miracles*, called "A Wood." She wrote to me in October of that year to propose doing "another one together. How do you like this as an opening line? "My rhumba teacher is forever proposing marriage. This is ridiculous since I'm already married." Unfortunately I don't seem to have leapt on this invitation—I met the man who would become my husband shortly after that, so perhaps I was distracted by courtship.

Nicholas and I have chosen the letters below from among the many letters of advice she sent to student writers, mainly through the Humber program, that we found in the archives—Carol printed and kept copies of the letters as she sent them. (We have removed identifying information.) The problems and issues she describes in the manuscripts she was reviewing are common, if not universal, and her advice would serve anyone who is writing or planning to write. Her thoughts on "thickening" come up often as she encouraged her correspondents toward "thickening, explaining, describing, taking it slowly, letting the pages breathe. And occasionally going in a little deeper, a sudden plunge that takes the reader by surprise."

January 11, 1995
Carol to AG

Can you provide me with a project plan? Are you committed to short stories or would you really rather be working on a novel? I do understand that the size of the work can be worrying, but novels are written in small scenes, just as stories are. The question is one of density, I think. I also think you should ask yourself what you like to read, novels or stories? (I always believe in writing the book you want to read.)

January 31, 1995
Carol to KA

You say you store opening lines. Are you saying you want to put your greatest emphasis on those lines? Atwood says she builds her poems around one line, and that line can occur anywhere in the poem. If you look at her work you can often find it; it is a line that uses words in a striking sequence, where the compression startles and illuminates.

In [your poem] why not use the description you wrote in your letter, the tears flying out like missiles. This is far more powerful than the slow rolling tears in the poem.

I wouldn't worry about punctuation. But you might want to remember that its = possession and it's = it is. You're quite right that line breaks and space do the work [in poetry] that punctuation does in prose. Periods and commas mostly come up like clutter in poems (my opinion, not shared by all). I wouldn't worry about grammar too much either, you can catch that later. It is important, though, to avoid "poetic" words, pretty words, archaic words and any thought that doesn't feel fresh.

What to do when new thoughts surface in a poem you're writing? This would vary, but it might add all kinds of richness to put them in. There's no reason a poem has to be linear. Diversions can illuminate as well as distract, and they can give a kind of randomness and texture that feels like truth.

You say your work merits a nod or a laugh, but don't you really want more; don't you want your reader to say, "Aha, I've felt exactly that way too, but I've never seen it articulated."

I remember being shocked that Sylvia Plath used a thesaurus when writing poetry; it sounds so, well, unpoetic. But she's good at finding the exact word, a different word, a word that's full of allusive power.

February 6, 1995
Letter from Carol Shields to CZ

You ask if there is one problem that beginning writers share, and that brings me to my big point. The most common problem, after clichés or point of view, is the use of too many underdeveloped scenes.

I do like your terseness, but feel that the scenes need to be longer; they need to be set up, fully furnished, given an "atmosphere," then trusted. You can stay in the scene as long as it's still yielding up something useful for you, and you can expand the scene by dialogue, by description, by the use of side-stories, and especially by giving us the content of the person's head, the thoughts, reflections, responses. This leads to much thicker writing, but I think you can still keep your crispness. An example is the scenes on the ship. We need more of the atmosphere of a tour ship, the smells, the daily schedules. You talk about art classes; what else is offered? You have the dinner scenes, but not much else. Who else is on this cruise? What is the weather like? Where is it anyway? I suggest that you double this chapter. And that you get it solidly in place before you go on with your draft. I don't have much sense of the sister here either, other than that she's beautiful. What does she do all day on the ship? Who is paying for this trip? She sounds, perhaps, too nice. I gather she's a widow—do we need to know more?

In the second chapter, I don't always feel secure in time and space. Where is their house, what kind of neighbourhood? How "comfortable" are they? I find it odd that she's thinking of leaving him, because I don't quite understand if she's just bored or fed up or if there's more going on here. The children don't feel as though they're really there. I guess I don't understand this household reality, but I think I would if you'd thicken the details and give me more.

I don't plot my novels really. I have a sense of where I'm going, but I don't know how I'll get there. I do assign myself a structure though. I think of it as raw boxes (chapters) that I'll fill with SOMETHING. I always know how many chapters I'll have and what the time period will be. But that's about all.

February 6, 1995
Carol to KA

Poetry, it seems to me, needs to be terse, elliptical, allusive rather than "on the nose" in its content.

I also want to comment on a few things you mentioned in your letter. You say you read to learn 'why my life wasn't the same as others'." This strikes me as a profound theme, and one you might work with. I suppose this is what we all do, but you've said it clearly. It has the midnight ring of truth to it. I wouldn't worry—at this point—about being confessional. In a sense all writing is confessional. The trick is to be personal but not private in the kind of writing.

You say the "words just come, almost from my subconscious." My sense is that this can be a problem. A poem, even free verse, is shaped and somewhere in the poem there needs to be a line or two that gestures toward the poet's deliberation. We need to see a thought not tossed out, but formed. Poetry needs to feel natural, that is, use the language we speak, but it very seldom comes out as we speak or think.

February 19, 1995
Carol to KV

I'm rushing this back to you after a single reading because the mail seems very slow between Canada and Tokyo; I've no doubt the delay is with Canada.

First, I do thank you for your warm words of praise. Second, I think you have some wonderful, rare and exotic material that should help you find a publisher and an audience. I urge you to make the most of this "special" material, explaining and commenting on it, never losing sight of its strangeness.

Your central question—can a western person ever fully comprehend an eastern way of thinking?—is an interesting and compelling one, and it might be useful if you raise it right away. (You can always take it out later if it seems too intrusive.) And you might want to try to find a way to rephrase this question in every chapter; this will help you keep it in focus, and help this reader know your direction.

Your questions on the back of page II indicate that you already grasped the most worrying areas. If you have a problem, I would think it would be pacing. Yes, you do have an awful lot in chapter I. The fire, and the loss of her career seem to be over far too quickly. So, perhaps, is her parting from S. You can make her more reflective, more humorous about her passions, more confused about her future.

March 10, 1995
Carol to KA

I've just reread your letter and want to respond to a couple of points. The difference between "tossed out" and "formed"—the 5th stanza of [your poem], the final four lines: these feel shaped to me, containing the naturalness of speech but indicating a kind of torque you've put on the words. They leap out, something shaped, the way the word "falls" leans toward the word "mausoleum," for instance, and the way the word "weight" connects with "heavily" both logically and in terms of sound.

I was interested in what you said about your generation being conditioned to expect immediate return for attention. This has always seemed to me the difference between prose and poetry: that poetry must go off like a flashbulb. No I don't think you need to educate your reader, but you do need to provide the flash, and perhaps you're right that surprising language gets in the way. It is really the way one word is placed surprisingly against another that sets off the flash, not verbal eccentricity.

And, no, I don't think terseness always pays its way. "Summer through the back door comes flying" is rich in its long opening line, made me think of Whitman's "Lilacs."

Two things in your letter suggested ideas for future poems you might consider. One: your notion that you had nothing to say for a long time. Could you write about this? And how you found out that you did have something to say. And two, your suggestion that you feel you should be "nice"—I urge you to not be concerned with niceness in what you write but perhaps to write about the struggle with niceness. (And, oh brother. I've had that struggle.)

April 2, 1995
Carol to KV

It was good to hear from you and see where you had gone since the last mailing.

First, let me say this seems to be going along well. It might be interesting to see E's thoughts go back to the US occasionally, and all she left behind. I would try to pattern in these thoughts, maybe once every third page or so. Does this sound too artificial to you?

I've marked a variety of suggestions. V.p. means vague pronoun. I always know what you mean, but think you should reorganize the sentence so that there is not even a shred of ambiguity.

You'll see I marked a few awkward sentences—they work grammatically, but gave me "pause."

And I've suggested breaking up quotations several times. This mainly makes it easier on the reader, keeping track of the speaker, and the tone of the speech.

These are small points. My big point is that I am wondering if you should consider shifting W's speech patterns. I know what you're doing, really I do—you want to give the flavour of his speech. But sometimes this has the effect of pigeon English, and might even be unintentionally comic. You might need to ask yourself: how do I want the reader to perceive this man? He is wise and intelligent; and you want, I think, to show him that way. If you have him speaking a formal and correct English, rather than broken English, you may be twisting the linguistic truth, but you will also be using a convention that is well understood and, I think, generally well accepted by readers. My feeling is that this is important—at this point in the novel—to consider. Please give me your thoughts on this issue. I'm probably dead wrong.

I'll look forward to reading more. Interesting your comments on Shirley and New Age. These distinctions are not understood here—not generally anyway.

When I write "really?" I'm just reacting to the information. Saying to you: is this true? I think you mean it to be taken as true. Right?

The letter is just right.

The pacing is fine too. You've slowed it down, good.

All good wishes.

April 17, 1995
Carol to AG

I've made a few scratches—hope that's okay—pointing out places
where I thought you had commented, unnecessarily, on what you
had already made clear. The writing stays crisper if you can resist
explaining, and I think most of your material stands up without it.

Everyone organizes their writing differently, but I think you
should definitely keep on doing what you're doing—writing short
scenes and not worrying too much at this point how they're going
to fit together. Keep sending them to me as soon as you have a
few—though it's better to send by mail than fax, since our one
fax machine serves the whole Arts building and it is guarded by a
rather dour soul.

Your short scenes work well, though some of them need setting
up in time and space, just a hint or two at the top of each one. And
I needed to know Pepper was a woman much sooner.

As you pile up your scenes, you may find you want to deepen
them occasionally, and that you can do this without jolting the
rhythm—letting us know, for instance, that S is not just dateless,
but deeply lonely...

June 18, 1995
Carol to ML

Most of the things I've mentioned before: the repetition of words
and whole phrases. Sometimes I think this is accidental and
sometimes I believe you do it for effect, building to a crescendo.

I think it could look like a stylistic tic, and could weary or exasperate the reader. I've marked most of these places, suggesting that you rework the sentences so that you reach the desired force in another way.

It seems to me, too, that there's an overuse of semicolons and colons. I suggest that every time you find yourself using one, you stop and see if you can restructure the sentence so you don't need one. (Ed Carson gave me this advice years ago, and I bless him.) Their occasional use can be very effective.

Some passages need tightening in order to keep the reader reading, and I've marked most of them. Mostly it's a case of excessive detail, accuracy served but rhythm and interest sacrificed.

August 14, 1995
Carol to IL

Your letter with its questions and observations was like a little essay on writing, and I enjoyed it enormously. I think I fall on the intuitive side of writing, not always knowing everything about my characters, and often not really knowing what a story or even a novel is ABOUT. On the other hand, I don't believe stories write themselves or that characters "take over." (When people talk about these things, I think they're really saying that one has released the imagination a little. Someone wrote me this week to ask what happened to Maria in *The Stone Diaries*, and I had to confess I didn't know for sure.) Write about what you know, people say, but how do you know what you know?

I would like to tell you to forget you are the granddaughter of a Baptist preacher, but I doubt if you can and would worry what the cost might be. I am convinced that the Methodist Sunday School—all those years!—will be with me forever, even though I no longer have my formal beliefs. A large part of me admires reticence, seeing it as kind of a writerly tact or, as the divine Emily says, a way of preventing blindness ("tell all the truth but tell it slant"). Not so different from your word: oblique. What I try for is pushing against the form while staying inside it, making for myself a kind of tension that I can control. (Does this make any sense?) I love this notion of being "ready to testify," but think that probably we "testify" with every word, or with every act.

In Alice Munro's stories, there is often a sentence near the end of the piece, never at the end, or rarely, in which she tells the reader, fairly directly, what the story is about. I look for these. It occurred to me you might bury in your story a rather striking remark you made in your letter, about the affair and the abuse being concurrent rather than one causing the other. Can you find a way to say that?

August 16, 1995
Carol to QE

An interesting story. I have a couple of suggestions, and the more important one is that you try putting this story into past tense—which will give you, I think, a richer sense of narrative. You may find your sentences growing longer and more reflective, and I think the story needs this to give it resonance.

I like the first person, and think it can, if you let it, give voice
to your concern about political correctness. You can say exactly
what you said to me in your letter, let out your feelings, your
reflections. Again, I think this will make the story richer.
We need to trust the intelligence of that first person voice. As it is,
it seems a little jaunty and off-hand.

August 21, 1995
Carol to IU

Hello after the long summer. Hope you had a good lazy time of it
and weren't too much affected by the US heat wave.

I'm sending back about fifty edited pages, and will try to get
another batch off to you in the next week or two.

I'm a little concerned about the "sprawl" of the novel, since
it's very tricky to knit together so many strands. I love the "apple"
material, but in some ways it sounds like another whole novel. It's
very detailed, and it moves a long way back in time. I don't want
to discourage you; you did tell me your overall design, but I think
you've chosen a hard-to-control multiple narrative. On the other
hand, you may find when you get it all roughly in place, that you
can go back and make some needed connections and transitions,
and that the novel is all the richer for your ambitious scheme.

I do urge you to work more on the level of the sentence, and I
suggest that the best way to do this is to read the material aloud,
once, twice, whatever it takes. Trust your ear. Some of the sections are made up of short choppy sentences that perhaps can
be brought together, giving rhythm and coherence. A number of

sentences are lacking verbs (I've marked some of these, though not all). I realize you are suggesting the unfinished structure of interior thought, but some of it seems unnecessarily awkward, and quite a few sections gave me "pause." Again, I feel you can pick this up by reading aloud. I mean *really* out loud, too, not just in your head. I suggest, at this point, keeping an eye on mechanical problems too; spelling, punctuation, vague pronouns.

I like L's thoughts about her aging body, her reworking of her life, why she is the way she is. Interesting material. K still feels a little vague to me, but perhaps she will open in the next section.

All best wishes with this. Let me know your thoughts.

August 22, 1995
Carol to IB

Yes, I think the names work much better now. I do keep my chapters in separate files in the computer (but it's only the last book I wrote on the computer). And I have another file for the chapter titles themselves. I'm rather eccentric in that I almost always decide early on how many chapters I'm going to have and their approximate length. I visualize them as little boxes. I'm going to fill a little train of boxes (or else hangers on a coat rack) though I don't know what's going in them (or on them). I did give the chapters names, usually names on a time line: Birth, Childhood, etc. With my first novel, *Small Ceremonies*, I have each chapter the name of a month in the academic year. I think it helps keep you organized to have titles, even though you may want to abandon them later.

August 26, 1995
Carol to IU

Some more pages returned. Most of my suggestions are in the text, and many are the same as when I last wrote. You are using a lot of dashes, and I think that if you resist you'll find ways to make more interesting and varied sentences. I think your sentences are where you need to concentrate your energy. Some of your details of the natural world are lovely and highly precise, and you might try to bring that kind of care to the interior life of your characters.

If you read your work aloud you should be able to get a feel for when you need to use a name or a pronoun. Or when, in dialogue, you need to use names in address.

I suggest rethinking Chapter 23. Can this information be compressed and inserted in another chapter? You aren't really obliged to fill in every character's background, parentage, courtship, etc., and I am worried that you're getting far away from the main lines of the story. Let me know what you think.

Shall send some more pages next week.

All best

August 27, 1995
Carol to AG

I found your pages, as always, fun to read, lively, full of social comment. I haven't yet seen enough to know where all this is going. Most of my suggestions in the text deal with mechanical problems. Where I've written v.p., vague pronoun, I'm really suggesting that you restructure the whole sentence, looking for new ways to avoid certain words: "just," in particular. It's hardly ever needed. Writers talk about something called the "somehow syndrome." The use of "somehow" usually means you haven't thought it through. I've also marked problems with tense and with certain repeated sentence structures. I guess I really do believe that writing succeeds or fails at the level of the sentence. I suggest you read your work out loud, really out loud, not just in your head. You'll soon hear where these repeated structures fall, and also those places where the language could be fresher, more original.

I caution you against making these people "types," instead giving them certain inconsistencies, moment of redemption, flashes of self-doubt, reflection. Don't be afraid to expand; you can always cut back later.

August 28, 1995
Carol to ML

I've marked a variety of things, repeated words, very occasional awkwardness, and particularly, places where I think you've been slightly over rigorous in your use of precise detail. I love detail, particularly when it attaches to sensory experience, but there were places here where it seemed to serve nothing. You'll see what I mean, I think.

September 19, 1995
Carol to AG

I'm returning these pages with some scribbled comments, most of
which seem to fall into the following categories:

1. Varying structure. I've marked some, and you'll pick up
    others. You can start by joining some of the shorter sentences,
    trying to keep them aloft grammatically—and through this
    you should discover new and more interesting structures.
    You can also make a deliberate attempt to start sentences
    with prepositional clauses. I suggest you read your favourite
    writers and see how they do it. I honestly believe that writing
    succeeds or fails at the sentence level.

2. I think you need to "thicken" your scenes, and you already do
    this by way of dialogue. But you can also use more sensory
    description of people, their faces, their clothes, their gestures,
    their surroundings, but particularly—and I think this is most
    important—what they are thinking. I need, for instance, to
    know how these characters feel about their new-age thera-
    pists. I feel a sense of mockery, and yet they seem to take their
    advice seriously. Is there conflict there as I sense? I think you
    have to make up your mind about the narrator's tone toward
    the characters and toward the material. Every scene could be
    twice as long as it is.

3. I've been thinking about what I miss in these characters and I
    think I've finally put my finger on it. You can do what you want
    with them, make them good, silly, mean, whatever, but I think
    we have to know that you, the writer, honour and like (love?)

them. It may seem ridiculous to speak in these terms about a comic novel—and I think that's what this is—but even comedy needs characters we can feel for. And we can only feel for them if you feel for them.

Many of the things I've mentioned may be what you'll want to go back to when you've done your first draft. (Everyone arrives at a final draft differently.) But you might try—and I do suggest this—doing it as you write: thickening, explaining, describing, taking it slowly, letting the pages breathe. And occasionally going in a little deeper, a sudden plunge that takes the reader by surprise.

September 21, 1995
Carol to AG

My comments—mostly noted in the margins—have to do with sentence structure, sentence variation, tense changes. This may seem boring stuff, but writing lives and dies at the sentence level. I suggest you work on longer and more varied sentences; you already have the knack of the short ones. Try beginning sentences with prepositional phrases; try adding clause on clause and see if you can get more power, maybe even more lyrical rhythm.

I also suggest that you "thicken" your scenes. Tell us about the weather, set up the scene in terms of the time of day, the furniture. You already have a lot of food—perhaps too much, though you do it very well.

September 21, 1995
Carol to A

I'm returning your poem with a few suggestions, though I'm not awfully good at this. I love it, actually, particularly the changing form of the obituary. One thought was to try to establish the narrator's identity a little earlier (the fact that "you" is really "I") but I'm not sure how you can do this without getting heavily into narrative. I was a little confused by this, and then had to scramble to readjust. In the bottom of page 2, you can separate the two stories by using separate stanzas, but this leaves it a little late.

I do think you have a story collection now, and that you needn't necessarily wait to get more stories published. Do you have some ideas of where to go for publication? I'd be happy to write a supporting letter when you do decide—let me know.

Anne Lamott has written a book called *Bird by Bird* about writing. I haven't read it, but I attended a reading she did in California and I thought she was brilliant. But these books can confuse one with their conflicting advice. My advice—you didn't ask, but here it comes—is to write "thick." You can always prune later. This and loose, far looser than with short stories, just let it pour forth, piling it up. The other thing to remember is that if you write one page a day, you'll have a novel in a year. It helps—at least it helps me—to set out my chapters in the beginning, some kind of timeline. I wrote the first novel by deciding it would cover the nine months of the academic year, and each chapter was to be a month. I didn't know what was going into the chapters, but this structure, somehow, kept me on track.

You asked about movies. *Swann* is being filmed right now in Toronto, with Brenda Fricker and Miranda Richardson starring. Also a beautiful young man from *Twin Peaks* whose name I can't remember. I went for the first read-through, though I'm not really involved and didn't write the script. I was full of skepticism, but to my surprise it was incredibly exciting.

A, it's been wonderful working with you. You are a gifted writer, full of ideas and willing to take real risks. (Bold is a very good word to remember when writing.) Part of the pleasure of doing this Humber course has been connecting with women writers that I now think of as friends. That's been a lovely surprise. Keep in touch.

December 1, 1995
Carol to KA

I read this with great pleasure. It is suffused with warmth, and is accessible without being simplistic, and the narrator/letter writer is thoroughly likeable. I feel you did an excellent job of pacing, releasing the background about the marriage slowly, taking your time. And I like the way you brought in subtly the mother's possible unhappiness, the limitations of the life she lived. You did the same with the third sister, just hinting at the relationships.

I think you might have missed an opportunity of a counter-narrative: mentioning the substance of J's life, her letters. It is something to think about anyway.

There is a problem with this kind of narrative strategy—how do you give information to someone who mostly has it already? J knows much of this background, so I suggest you say more frequently things like "you'll remember how we" or "this is old stuff to you but" or "I don't have to remind you of how Dad" etc. etc. There are all kinds of structure you can use.

I suggest loosening up the prose so that it's more letterly, more sisterly, less formal. You can use more contractions for one thing, and more informal speech. And I do suggest dropping semicolons, since they are generally thought of as quite formal.

And I also suggest "thickening." More descriptions, more sensory details, how people look, their names, the weather, how things smell. More concrete details.

March 2, 1996
Carol to ZQ

I admire the poems not just for their technique, but for the way they branch out to ideas. (I've always thought that each poem should contain an idea, and yours do, except for "Snow," which seems all image, a sort of haiku feeling to it, and "Stones," which I don't understand.) I confess I also like them because they seem joyous and, in an entirely unsoupy and intelligent way, optimistic.

March 20, 1996
Carol to LG

This is all most fascinating! Your stories from the Bank are shaping, as they used to say in Manchester. (By the way, my time in the North of England in the early sixties helps me to accept the reality of what you have on the page here; otherwise I think I might have doubted the horror and the structure of these trapped lives.)

You have made powerful the nightmare of everyday life, and, curiously, at the same time have redeemed that life. Quite an accomplishment. Your blind doll of a child in the midst of the tangled chaos is extraordinary though—lovely in every way.

Most of my comments have to do with adjectival or adverbial overload, which weaken rather than strengthen the effect I think you want. I've suggested cuts; most of these move toward a crisper, sharper (I think) image. Occasionally whole clauses can be rethought: do you need them? I've written "tighten" in these cases but really mean "rethink." How can you say what you want to say more cleanly, more economically?

You do a good job of getting inside M's head, and so I don't think you always need your "She thought." Once you're there, you're there.

I think that this time you've got a sense of local usage without sacrificing clarity or eliciting head scratching.

Once or twice—and I've marked these places—I sensed an abrupt shift of tone.

One danger you might want to watch out for in the future is a romanticizing of G. There is a tendency to dehumanize labour leaders in literature, fill their mouths with speeches and lose their individual and human sense.

Your postcard story is charming with a strong sense of voice.

A wonderful project, L. I am excited by it.

March 26, 1996
Carol to KA

I read this with pleasure. The idea is breathtaking: lives that themselves straddle three centuries, and then all attached lives that are making the (purely abstract) jump. I wonder how many three-century souls there will be—more than a handful, I expect.

I kick myself for missing the discussion, since there are so many questions. Does this represent your whole project, or is it a part of a larger piece? How did you select your people? What, if you could put it succinctly, are you saying about the artificiality of time?

You have some nice scenes here. I love the journalist in H—a good device with a nice satirical edge. I was drawn, too, to the young boy trying so hard to be good at the seniors' home. We don't often see this straining toward goodness in fiction. I was also very interested in the case of extreme shyness and wish you'd gone further with it somehow—why are people cripplingly shy and how do they bear it? Can you find a way to tie this in with the idea of time?

In fact, I think you might have expanded almost everywhere. I've marked places where I think you could, for instance, be more concrete, give examples, and provide more substance to a scene. But you might push further, too, in terms of what people are thinking.

You've chosen to use a number of run-on (comma splice) sentences; sometimes these work for me, giving a sense of breathless narrative, almost stream of consciousness. Sometimes, though, they look like mistakes.

I've marked a number of sentences that for one reason or another seem awkward. Sometimes it's grammar getting in the way, or vague pronouns (v.p.), but mostly it strikes me that you simply need to rethink them, reorder them. You might try reading them out loud, and then, if you can hear the bumpiness, attempt an alternate structure or even several possibilities.

This piece, with revision, should find publication (I think, hope).

All good wishes.

March 26, 1996
Carol to AA

I've always believed fiction to be about redemption, about trying to see why people are the way they are. When we talk about women of a certain age, we often dismiss them as the "blue rinse girls" or the "white glove ladies," failing to imagine their inner lives, the million differences that make each of them unique. I wanted Mrs. Turner, with all her particles of differences, to shine.

April 2, 1996
Carol to KP

I have a dozen questions for you, as I think the class will.

How much have you actually written? I'm not sure how this connects with the first term project, the juncture that is. I would like to know—if you know—where you're going with this. How much of a hero do you want to make of F or do you intend any such thing? What do the people in the story want, and are their desires located in the "real" world or in fantasy?

This is richly imagined; I'm not sure though that you've coloured in all the connections yet. Your handling of dialogue, especially extended dialogue, is excellent—I can feel the tension growing and each exchange moves it forward.

I like the fact that you've created a whole world, or perhaps appropriated a whole world. Some of the details of the fantasy life are fascinating, and you've made it solid.

For me, the main problem was confusion. Where are we in time and space and who is doing what? I was constantly off balance. You have a lot of people, a number of levels of "reality," some of your characters have two names. This is a good deal to ask of a reader. In addition, there is the chunk of narrative we haven't seen. I think you could do much to clarify the story if you were more careful about vague pronouns, marked v.p. in the text. We need these tags so we don't have to keep reading back and also so we know that YOU know WHO is Who. What I'm talking about is more "authority" from the author, and often you do this well.

I think you might ask yourself what, in a phrase, is your main through line. And are you able to keep this through line firmly at the front of the narrative. Is it F's quest? If so, what is that quest?

Looking forward to discussion.

April 2, 1996
Carol to K

This is very funny, very engaging; I hated for it to end.

You've got off quickly with a bang of an opening, fooling us into thinking we were in for dullness, then pulling the rug out. Lovely. You've done a good job conveying the kind of boredom that would make these kinds of games inevitable. And the phone sex itself is hilarious; I only wish you'd provided just a bit more, rather than suggesting to us where the conversation went. But it works well. Very visual, very nice. Curiously innocent, which is also nice.

Occasionally I wanted other bits thickened a bit, particularly the setting. And a little more attention to who is speaking. I sometimes had to reach back.

Where should this go? I don't think you want to lose the lightness, but you could darken it slightly—you've read Lorrie Moore, so you will know what I mean. What does it mean that one person manipulates another, even in fun? Is anyone hurt, anyone punished? I can only imagine a kind of ironic doubling back, a genuine erotic passion growing in the place of this rehearsed one. But would a lawyer and a cowboy be able to—? You'd have to give it legs, somehow. Anyway, I love it. And with revision, clarification, closure, can see it being published so that other people can love it. I look forward to hearing the class suggestion for an ending.

Hope you had a good holiday.

December 16, 1996
Carol to AG

I'm going to get off a few impressions with the manuscript and
will send more later when I've had time to digest my feelings.
I certainly loved what you did at the end, and think, with a few
revisions, you could do Chapter 12 as a short story and send it to
the *New Yorker*. You'd have to get rid of P though. I don't know
how you knew how someone this sick would feel, making that final
effort. Marvellous.

The whole book is a fine accomplishment, and I think will find
its audience. It's often amusing.

I suggest a few things. One, that you stop from time to time and
summarize: Something like—This is P's last year of exploration,
her daughter is sick and in crisis, her son is emerging from sexual
ambiguity and finding a connection. I notice that many writers do
this, and that it helps keep everything on track.

Two, that you try to get rid of some of your parentheses. I know
why you have them: because there is an undervoice to so much of
the novel. But the material doesn't need commenting on. Even if
you eliminated half of them—

I would love to have had one mention of the potluck club—a
paragraph or two—in each chapter, as a sort of binding together
mechanism.

The only place I lost interest was during some of the dreams. I
think it was John Barth who cautioned his students about the use
of dreams in novels, that we are interested in our own dreams but

not necessarily in others'. How important are they to the unwinding of P's journey? Perhaps you could telescope them slightly.

Some of the pronouns were unclear—and I've marked those. In most cases it's easier just to reconstruct the sentence.

It's been a joy to read this, B. You never make P cute or, god forbid, feisty. Perhaps you could have her reflect now and then about how she's doing fulfilling the role of "older person." Is she good at it? Is she resisting, going along with it?

Will it ever stop snowing!

Undated
Carol to Q

This is a fine project. Your introduction opened up some personal issues which would be interesting to discuss: Hélène Cixous and her theory of writing as liberation, writing as a way of bringing equality between the sexes, and your evident freedom and pleasure in writing in English rather than German—all three ideas interest me.

Overall I find your writing "blooming" in these pieces. The image that comes to mind is that of a "fountain overflowing." You are generous with yourself and indulgent with language (once or twice I think you went over the top, but then where is the top?). You use language, in any case, daringly, risking curious juxtapositions that almost always work. In this project, more than the last, I felt your English was solidly in place, but that would only be natural, I think.

Your mingling of domestic detail and life's larger emotions feels natural, unself-conscious. The laundry experience achieved humour in the face of frustration, and I liked YOUR stance in the piece, the baffled observer who is, nevertheless, determined to master the machine. You might want to take this piece a little deeper, widen it out slightly.

The persona of the narrator, you, is suggested with an ardent and contagious energy, with boundless curiosity, and, most interesting to me, a rare and natural tenderness toward the world.

I've made occasional marks: the odd awkward construction. Opaque (to me) references. Some images that don't work for me. Phrases that seemed to me unnecessary.

Undated
Carol to L

A good project. I can see you've spent time thinking your way through this, establishing character and setting up scenes. Your dialogue is funny, smart, quick, sure-handled. You use it to move the story forward as well as add texture. And you're generous with it.

I like your nice ironies: that A feels that she is unworthy of a handsome man, for instance. (Someone out there gets the handsome men.)

I've marked a few sentences that I think could do with a haircut.

And I have a suggestion: that you occasionally, for both A and E, provide a sudden deepening. An emotional deepening. I know that

you are working on a vein of romantic comedy—and not everyone can do this—but I don't believe you'd lose your tone, or your
footing, if you showed us, now and then, your characters' dark side.
Their very real insecurity. Their loneliness. You might, by letting
their banter merge with sudden sincerity, let us know how grateful
they are for each other's friendship. It sometimes helps if you ask
yourself: what does A want? (for instance) and let her speak to it,
even if she speaks only to herself.

I feel this growing toward a longer work, and look forward to
watching it.

Undated
Carol to L

You've done a lot of work on this, and large parts of it succeed. You
know how to show tenderness, and also humour, and your dialogue
is consistently good and believable.

I've marked a few problems, and chief of these is pacing. The
Paris interlude seemed to arrive too quickly, and never really
establishes itself in my mind. (I didn't feel much in the section that
spoke of the flavour of Paris. You might do more with Montréal
too—name neighbourhoods. Describe her journey to school and
back home every day. The seasons, the public gardens, the cafés
and theatres and shops.) And I was unsure how long the various
episodes lasted. It's important to keep the reader solidly located in
time as well as in space.

I've marked passages, too, where the language goes suddenly
stiff and formal and out of joint with the nice, loose feeling of
the rest.

You get into S's point of view very occasionally. Consider carefully whether you need to do this. And whether you want to. It might be much more effective to stay with A.

I need to know where you are going to from here. This isn't the end is it?

A good project. I do hope to see more. I'd like to know if she can really leave Carrot River (innocence) behind. Ask yourself: what does it mean to leave your past behind?

ACKNOWLEDGEMENTS

WE WISH TO THANK DONALD SHIELDS FOR HIS EARLY AND enthusiastic support of this project; the staff of Library and Archives Canada, including Catherine Hobbs, for their astute and thoughtful assistance in gathering the material collected here; Trena White and Jesse Finkelstein, of Page Two Strategies, who encouraged and supported our work from notion to publication; and Anne Collins and Amanda Lewis, of Penguin Random House Canada, who helped provide this book form and focus.

Thanks also to Freydis Welland for her invaluable insights, and to Bradley Dunseith and Anjalika Samarasekera for theirs, and to Dorothea Belanger and Marcy Zlotnick for their invaluable notes and memories of studying writing with Carol. Chapter 14 would not exist without their class notes.

Finally, we wish to thank Carol Shields for taking so many opportunities to shed light on the craft of writing, and for helping writers learn to notice things, to recognize a story when they see it, and to trust their impulses.

SOURCES

GENEROSITY, TIME AND FINAL ADVICE

Terry Gross interview: "Everyone asks me this…" Fresh Air, NPR, July 18, 2003, www.npr.org/templates/story/story.php?storyId=1340226.

CHAPTER ONE

"A View from the Edge of the Edge" in *Carol Shields and the Extra-Ordinary*, Marta Dvořák and Manina Jones, eds. (McGill-Queen's University Press, 2007); "Why Do Writers Write," speech, 1988; "The Case for Curling Up with a Book," essay, 1997; paper, undated.

"I've always seemed to be able…" Undated letter to Anne Giardini.

"A good question…" An Interview with Carol Shields, BookBrowse, www.bookbrowse.com/author_interviews/full/index.cfm/author_number/764/carol-shields.

CHAPTER TWO

Paper on myths about writing, untitled, undated.

"And I have my writing..." *Unless* (Random House Canada, 2002), p. 2.

"Romance novels... are able to fill their pages..." *Unless*, pp. 206–7.

CHAPTER THREE

"Of Boxcars and Coat Hangers and Other Helpful Devices," paper, 1997.

"I thought I understood..." *Unless*, p. 13.

"Out of her young, questioning self..." *Jane Austen: A Life* (Penguin Group, 2001), p. 9.

CHAPTER FOUR

"Crossing Over," paper, 1990.

"I like to sketch in a few friends..." *Unless*, p. 122.

Peter Ward: "head-on into the frustration..." Publication unknown; attribution confirmed and permission obtained October 29, 2015.

CHAPTER FIVE

Creative Writing Courses, a lecture given in Trier, Germany, April 1990; *Scribner's Best of the Fiction Workshops*, Carol Shields, ed. (Simon & Schuster, 1998).

"To write is to be self-conscious..." *Jane Austen*, pp. 120–21.

"It had always seemed something of a miracle to him..." *Swann* (Random House Canada, 1987).

Writing Assignments: Creative writing notes, courtesy of D. Belanger and M. Zlotnick, English 4.350, University of Manitoba, 1994–1995.

CHAPTER SIX

"The Subjunctive Self," paper, undated.

"For every writer the degree of required social involvement..." *Jane Austen*, p. 119.

"Notes for Novel..." *Small Ceremonies* (McGraw-Hill Ryerson, 1976), pp. 55–56.

"A life is full of isolated events..." *Unless*, p. 313.

"Nevertheless, publication meant having a public self..." *Jane Austen*, p. 148.

"I work on my sonnets at a small keyhole desk..." "Segue" in *The Collected Stories* (Random House Canada, 2005), p. 11.

Letters of Sigmund Freud, Sigmund Freud, ed.; translated by Tania and James Stern (Basic Books, Inc.: 1960).

CHAPTER SEVEN

"On Avoiding Standards," paper, undated.

"There is a problem all fiction writers must face..." *Unless*, pp. 139–40.

"Where, then, did Jane Austen find the material..." *Jane Austen*, p. 70.

"... there is what the literary tribe calls a 'set piece'" "Flitting Behavior" in *The Collected Stories*, p. 80.

"The Seaside Houses," *The Stories of John Cheever* (Ballantine: 1946).

CHAPTER EIGHT

"Carol Shields" in *22 Provocative Canadians: In the Spirit of Bob Edwards,* Kerry Longrpré and Margaret Dickson, eds.; foreword by Catherine Ford, pp. 26–31; "Others," paper, undated; "Gender Crossing," talk, Canadian Booksellers Association, 1997.

CHAPTER NINE

"The Love Story," paper, undated.

"To be a romantic..." *The Republic of Love* (Vintage Canada, 1992).

CHAPTER TEN

Talk, Manitoba Writers' Guild, September 1994.

"I had an argument with Matt Cohen..." Undated letter to Anne Giardini.

"But we *have* to notice..." *The North British Review*, Volume XIX, May–Aug. 1853.

"The house seems to take up..." *Letters between Katherine Mansfield and John Middleton Murray*, Cherry A. Hankin, ed. (New Amsterdam Books: 1991).

"How wonderful it feels..." *Loitering with Intent* (The Bodley Head: 1981).

CHAPTER ELEVEN

"The New New New Fiction," paper, undated.

CHAPTER TWELVE

"Narrative Hunger and the Overflowing Cupboard," paper, undated; *Narrative Hunger, and the Possibilities of Fiction*, Edward Eden and Dee Goertz, eds. (University of Toronto Press, 2003).

"Years ago I belonged to a small writing group..." *Unless*, p. 271.

"Writing is mere writing..." Annie Dillard, *The Writing Life* (Harper & Row: 1989).

CHAPTER THIRTEEN

"A View from the Edge of the Edge."

"Having Lived in Chicago..." "As for Me and My House," *Books in Canada*, Jan.–Feb. 1985.

CHAPTER FOURTEEN

Creative writing notes, courtesy of Belanger and Zlotnick; Letter from Carol Shields to Anne Giardini, February 2, 1989.

"I have no idea what will happen in this book..." *Unless*, p. 16.

INDEX

Note: "CS" = Carol Shields

Calasso, Roberto, 97
Calisher, Hortense, 132
Callaghan, Morley, 137
Cambridge Movement, 57–58
Canada, 135. *See also* writing,
    Canadian
Canada Council, 138, 139
Carson, Ed, 159
Cartland, Barbara, 18
characters, 89–90, 177
    developing, 141, 146, 155, 159,
        164, 165
    in new new new fiction, 112, 145
Cheever, John, 77
Chekhov, Anton, 97–98
children (as subjects), 51
Cixous, Hélène, 175
cliché, 44, 77, 110–11, 141, 146
climax, 78, 80–81
Cohen, Matt, 99
Collins, Anne, xix (note)
colons, 159
conflict/resolution approach,
        26–28, 67–68, 110
    as male-centric, 27, 98
    need for, 98, 129, 145
Conrad, Joseph, 5
context, 69–71, 79, 127–28
    cultural, 148, 155
    establishing, 158, 172, 177
contractions, 146, 168
*Courtship, Love, and Marriage in
    Nineteenth-Century English
    Canada* (Ward), 35
Crabtree, Mabel, 11
craziness, 112, 144

creative process, 59, 62, 63–64
creative writing programs, 11, 38–41
    exercises for, 43, 46–48
    marking in, 44–45
    in *Small Ceremonies*, 40–41
    students of, 37, 39, 41, 43, 45
    teachers of, 39
crime novels, 67
crisis. *See* conflict/resolution
    approach
critics, 20, 103, 106
curiosity, 84–86
cutting, 79, 146. *See also* thickening
    of details, 72, 158, 164
cynicism, 132

Darnton, Robert, 124
David Copperfield (Dickens), 137
Davies, Robertson, 131, 145
DeLillo, Don, 59
dénouement, 78, 81
description, 147, 165. *See also* details
details (of other lives), 84–85
    cutting, 72, 158, 164
    embracing, 28–30, 72, 177
    importance of, 35–36, 86
    presenting, 147, 176
    in short stories, 97–98
    as thickening device, 73, 153, 171
Dewar's Scotch Whisky, 117–18
dialogue, 79–80, 146, 163
    consistency in, 157
    identifying speaker, 173
    informal speech in, 168
    as thickening device, 74
diaries, 35, 127

The Works of Carol Shields

Poetry
Coming to Canada
Intersect
Others

Novels
Unless
Larry's Party
The Stone Diaries
The Republic of Love
A Celibate Season (with Blanche Howard)
Swann
A Fairly Conventional Woman
Happenstance
The Box Garden
Small Ceremonies

Story Collections
Collected Stories
Dressing Up for the Carnival
The Orange Fish
Various Miracles

Plays
Unless
Thirteen Hands
Larry's Party—*the Musical*
(adapted by Richard Ouzounian with music by Marek Norman)
Anniversary: A Comedy (with Dave Williamson)
Fashion Power Guilt and the Charity of Families (with Catherine Shields)
Departures and Arrivals
Women Waiting

Criticism
Susanna Moodie: Voice and Vision

Biography
Jane Austen: A Life

Anthologies
Dropped Threads 2: More of What We Aren't Told
(edited with Marjorie Anderson)
Dropped Threads: What We Aren't Told
(edited with Marjorie Anderson)

BORN IN OAK PARK, ILLINOIS, IN 1935, CAROL SHIELDS MOVED TO Canada at the age of twenty-two, after studying at the University of Exeter in England, and then obtained her M.A. at the University of Ottawa. She started publishing poetry in her thirties, and wrote her first novel, *Small Ceremonies*, in 1976. Over the next three decades, Shields would become the author of over twenty books, including plays, poetry, essays, short fiction, novels, a book of criticism on Susanna Moodie and a biography of Jane Austen. Her work has been translated into twenty-two languages.

In addition to her writing, Carol Shields worked as an academic, teaching at the University of Ottawa, the University of British Columbia and the University of Manitoba. In 1996, she became chancellor of the University of Winnipeg. She lived for fifteen years in Winnipeg and often used it as a backdrop to her fiction, perhaps most notably in *The Republic of Love*. Shields also raised five children—a son and four daughters—with her husband, Don.

The Stone Diaries won a Governor General's Literary Award and a Pulitzer Prize, and was shortlisted for the Booker Prize, bringing Shields an international following. Her novel *Swann* was made into a film (1996), as was *The Republic of Love* (2003; directed by Deepa Mehta). *Larry's Party*, published in several countries and adapted into a musical stage play, won England's Orange Prize, given to the best book by a woman writer in the English-speaking world. And Shields' final novel, *Unless*, was shortlisted for the Booker, Orange and Giller prizes and the Governor General's Literary Award, and won the Ethel Wilson Prize for Fiction.

Carol Shields was always passionate about biography, both in her writing and her reading, and in 2001 she published a biography of Jane Austen. For Shields, Austen was among the greatest of novelists and served as a model: "Jane Austen has figured out the strategies of fiction for us and made them plain." In 2002, *Jane Austen* won the coveted Charles Taylor Prize for Literary Non-fiction. A similar biographical impulse lay behind the two *Dropped Threads* anthologies Carol Shields edited with Marjorie Anderson; their contributors were encouraged to write about those experiences that women are normally not able to talk about.

In 1998, Shields was diagnosed with breast cancer. Speaking on her illness, Shields once said, "It's made me value time in a way that I suppose I hadn't before. I'm spending my time listening, listening to what's going around, what's happening around me instead of trying to get it all down." In 2000, Shields and her husband Don moved from Winnipeg to Victoria, where they lived until her passing on July 16, 2003, from complications of breast cancer, at age sixty-eight.

ANNE GIARDINI, CAROL SHIELDS' DAUGHTER, HAS PUBLISHED two novels, *The Sad Truth about Happiness* and *Advice for Italian Boys*, and is working on a third.

NICHOLAS GIARDINI IS ONE OF CAROL SHIELDS' TWELVE GRAND-children. A committed reader, he enjoys books that explore character and self-perception.

Startle and Illuminate has been set in Janson, a misnamed typeface designed in or about 1690 by Nicholas Kis, a Hungarian in Amsterdam. In 1919 the original matrices became the property of the Stempel Foundry in Frankfurt, Germany. Janson is an old-style book face of excellent clarity and sharpness, featuring concave and splayed serifs, and a marked contrast between thick and thin strokes.